"GONE AWAY!"

THE DERRYDALE PRESS
FOXHUNTERS' LIBRARY

GONE AWAY

MASON HOUGHLAND, M.F.H.
with a new foreword by
MASON LAMPTON, M.F.H.

Foxes would get a great laugh

THE DERRYDALE PRESS
LANHAM AND NEW YORK

THE DERRYDALE PRESS

Published in the United States of America
by The Derrydale Press
4720 Boston Way, Lanham, Maryland 20706

Distributed by NATIONAL BOOK NETWORK, INC.

Copyright © 1949 BY THE BLUE RIDGE PRESS
First Derrydale Edition 2000

All rights reserved. No part of this publication may be reproduced,
stored in a retrieval system, or transmitted in any form or by any
means, electronic, mechanical, photocopying, recording, or otherwise,
without the prior permission of the publisher.
British Library Cataloguing in Publication Information Available

Library of Congress Cataloging-in-Publication Data

Houghland, Mason.
    Gone away / Mason Houghland.—1st Derrydale ed.
       p. cm.
    Originally published: Berryville, Va. : Blue Ridge Press, 1949.
    ISBN 1-58667-038-7 (cloth : alk. paper)—ISBN 1-56416-189-7 (leather : alk. paper)
    1. Fox hunting. 2.Foxhounds. I. Title
SK285.H83 2000
799.2'59775—dc21   00-063883

♾™ The paper used in this publication meets the minimum requirements of
American National Standard for Information Sciences—Permanence of
Paper for Printed Library Materials, ANSI/NISO Z39.48-1992.
Manufactured in the United States of America.

DEDICATION

This book is dedicated to,

SARA ROARK HOUGHLAND

without whose genius the beauty and pageantry of Hunting
and Hunt Racing in Tennessee might have been
but a shadow

Looking over the menu.

FOREWORD TO THE NEW EDITION

Mason Houghland was my maternal grandfather. He attained a reputation in England and America by writing and publishing *Gone Away*. This recognition in the world was unimportant to me as I was mesmerized by the man. He imprinted me with the knowledge that fun was to be found foxhunting. Foxhunting was to become the marriage of riding horses, hunting hounds, and enjoying the splendor of countless beautiful countrysides. It has led me to the people I have loved the most. This man instilled the magic or, as he said, the religion of the chase and all of its nuances.

Gone Away will give the reader a window on his passion for foxhunting. This book is a magnificent view of his personality, his professionalism as an author and huntsman, and most of all, his sense of humor. However, the reader is not able to glean from *Gone Away* the accomplishments of a young man's progress through life at the turn of the twentieth century. His life is a reflection of the final settlement of the west and two world wars. He was a student, soldier, husband, father, wildcatter for oil, founder of a successful business, huntsman, and writer. His story reflects a period that is gone. As he evolved into the man I came to know, one trait became his trademark: He endeared himself to those around him by the wonderful importance that he made of them.

Mason Houghland was born on the banks of the Ohio River near Rockport, Indiana, in 1888. His parents died at an early age. His family had a dry goods business, Houghland and Hardy, at the turn of the century which traded up and down the Ohio Valley. His father had been a partner in this enterprise, but the influence on young Mason's life was to be his Aunt Cordelia. She inspired him to attend West Point, which he quit due to math difficulties. From there he went to Stanford University. He would leave this school early as he took the side of the pro-alcohol contingent in a public debate. By his admission the debate got heated and he was asked to move elsewhere. The University of Chicago was the next stop, from which he graduated.

He worked hard on his math and became interested in geology and literature at these universities. During these years and following, he traveled the west looking for oil. He had hired on with Gulf Oil as a surveyor on horseback to search Wyoming. His letters describe the cowboys he met and the hunting of bear, coyote, and panthers. He wrote his sister about cowboy polo that he enjoyed playing on the ranches. During these games he played polo with the great comedian Will Rogers who left him with indelible memories.

With the outbreak of World War I he joined the cavalry and was assigned to Fort Riley, Kansas. His war record is unknown to me other than he had various assignments at posts stateside, and he left the service a Captain. It was while in Fort Riley that he met his wife to be, Sara Roark, an auburn-haired beauty who stole his heart. She was married to another officer, but that marriage came to an untimely end. Sara and Mason were wed after a torrid courtship. His letters to her are passionate. He pleads to the gods to have the mercy to melt her heart.

After World War I, Mason went west to make his fortune in oil. He was a wildcatter moving with his young family around the West in search of oil. He apparently had some success and some sickening disappointments. Some of his wells were successful, but their proceeds would be consumed as he drilled more dry holes. He and Sara had a daughter, Nancy (my mother). A son from Sarah's previous marriage, Calvin, was adopted by Mason. Nancy would tell of Mason entering their small home of several rented rooms in Ponca City, Oklahoma. He was covered with blood, and she, as a four-year-old child, was sure he had been scalped by the Indians. He had not been scalped, but he had killed a panther and had carried it home with great pride.

In his quest to find oil, he met John Paul Getty who left him one piece of wisdom the family has clung to: "Always hold back enough money to drill one more well." He finally left the wildcatting life and drove east across the Mississippi in a new Lincoln with his family and fifty dollars in his pocket, or so the family tale is told. An optimistic newcomer from the East had purchased his oil leases with cash.

With his stake, Mason drove to Nashville, Tennessee. He and Sara settled in a 1780's home that had endured Indian raids and the Battle of Franklin during the Civil War. The place was named "Green Pastures" after Psalm 23. They remained there until his death in 1959. It became a magnificent house for those who loved foxhunting, steeplechasing, and the keenest of wit. The place had hundred-year-old boxwood, monstrous magnolias, and an incredible library. On entering the grounds, the stable and kennel were off to the left about a quarter of a mile. The main drive crossed a large meadow with a stream and, ultimately, arrived at the house on a lovely knoll. The trees were old and magnificent. One big oak of at least 150 years had a hole through the center made by a cannon ball. The oak stood as a reminder of the Civil War battle that had raged on the seemingly peaceful ground.

Mason's settlement in Brentwood, Tennessee, was more than an address. He soon became a respected business leader. He sat on a bank board and became involved in the local issues. One of his most lasting contributions was the founding of the Iroquois Steeplechase. This was one of the only steeplechase meets dedicated to promote amateurism. The purse structure has always been at the top of the national scale. The course itself was built with men employed by the W.P.A., the public works program put forward by F. D. Roosevelt during the Great Depression. The race meet was chaired by his son Calvin for decades, to be succeeded by Henry Hooker, Joint-Master of the Hillsboro Hounds. Mason's son-in-law (my father), Dinwiddie Lampton Jr., won the inaugural running, followed two years later by Mason's son, Calvin, who had returned from the navy and World War II. The family was happily pulled into Mason's web of fun and gracious living. Sara lived up to the role of "Hostess Supreme," which allowed Mason to pursue this lifestyle with grace. This standard was set and followed by his get as they pursued their varied careers.

Mason needed to make some money on his arrival in Nashville. His family needed to be exposed to the world and savor its sweet nectar. He went to work on an idea that had sprung from his experience. He built gasoline stations and used the rail tanker cars as his means of supply which bypassed the high cost of trucking fuel from the rail depot to the gasoline station. He called his enterprise Spur Oil Company. This was a highly successful venture. In a quest for capital to expand his business, he raised what now is called venture capital. Von Opel of German automobile fame became one of Mason's investors. This became a terrible relationship while World War II raged as German possessions were confiscated during the war by the government. The repurchase of these shares put an incredible burden on Mason's young company. His financial relationship with Von Opel came to an end through a decision made by the United States Supreme Court.

While Mason was studying at college, wildcatting, and building Spur Oil Company, he loved to write. He had several stories published by the *Saturday Evening Post*. Many unpublished short stories are still in his files. He wrote and published *Gone Away*. In addition, after his death, Sara published his handwritten hunting diary.

His passion for foxhunting came into its full glory in Tennessee. He helped start the Harpeth Hills Hounds and then went on to found the Hillsboro Hounds. They were a Walker/English cross whose common characteristics included bidability, good cry, and white coloration. He loved white hounds because he could see them in the woods.

He loved his friends who populated all walks of society. Their common bond was their love for foxhunting. Sam Woolridge, a renowned night hunter and ladies man, was a great friend who sold him many Walker hounds. Woolridge advertised his hounds in *Chase Magazine* as "Walker Hounds with Woolridge Quality." Sam Woolridge joined Mason Houghland in the fun of the Kentucky State Field Trial, the National Trials, and others.

Joe Thomas, the great Master of the Piedmont Fox Hounds in Virginia and the author of *Hounds and Hunting through the Ages,* became his high priest of organized foxhunting. Mason joined with others to form the great Grasslands, a dream of Joe Thomas. It was in the middle of Tennessee and designed to host world championship polo, steeplechasing, and foxhunting. Paul Brown, the famous artist, painted the horses on the murals on the clubhouse walls. Famed portrait artists painted the people astride their mounts while landscape artists painted the hunt country in the background. Spending was unchecked, and the splendor of the club, built just before the Stock Market Crash of 1929, was unmatched. As you might imagine, after the Crash, the club disappeared but vestiges still remain. One of these murals went to Green Pastures after all the club's assets were put up for sale.

Mason Houghland was host to the North Cotswold foxhounds during the World War II years as a favor to his friend, Bill Scott. *The New York Times* wrote in grand style about the refugee pack as they landed on the wharf in Manhattan. In 1998 Bill Scott's son, Martin, a Master of the Vale of the White Horse, showed me the clippings of this incredible effort to save the pack carefully documented and maintained in several albums. Martin insists that after fifty years, I need to return the refugees in the form of Midland Hounds.

Mason found a hunting paradise in Wartrace, Tennessee. This town proudly proclaimed itself the Walking Horse capital of the world. The Walking Horse Hotel, just next to the rail station, became headquarters for some magnificent hunting memories. The country around Wartrace was unencumbered with wealth. There were no fences except split rail snake fences that were a joy to jump. Red foxes were everywhere. There was no way to run out of the country as it went on seemingly forever. Those white hounds would scream down the valley after his beloved "Red Ranger" joined by the stouthearted members of the Hillsboro. They would perform great deeds to be toasted around the fire at the Walking Horse Hotel.

Vernon Sharp, John Sloan, and John Harwell were Mason's key members. The former two would take over the mastership on his death. Billy Haggard was a member who would go on to ride in the Olympics. As a seven-year-old boy, I still recall my grandfather admiring a five-foot-six-inch gate that the great Haggard had just successfully leaped.

Children on ponies of various sizes descended on this village each Thanksgiving with excitement and mischief. The days' activities were well-filled. At four in the morning, breakfast was served. At dawn, the hunt cast. We hunted for many hours. An exhausted crew slept the afternoon to awaken in the evening and conceive terrorizing plans. Exploding fireworks, jumping on freight trains as they slowed in the station, and executing magnificent practical jokes were all part of our repertoire. These well-laid plans usually ran amuck under the watchful eyes of Big Mase as he was officially known by all children. The grandchildren,

Nana, Dinwiddie, Sara Jo, Mason Houghland Jr., Calvin Houghland Jr., and I, were joined by the children of many other families to include the Sloans, Sharps, Harwells, Davis', and many others. We were all following the Pied Piper.

The Sloan boys were a major part of his troop. Paul and George, especially, became students of how to love life. Big Mase would plead with John Sloan to allow the two boys to skip school to go hunting at early ages. Each became steeplechase riders of note. George Sloan, especially, became internationally renowned as an amateur steeplechase rider. He became the first American amateur to win the Leading Amateur title of England. The joy of hunting and coursing the countryside on a good horse was the lesson Big Mase wanted to teach his disciples.

This love for the children of the hunt would bear fruit. He instilled a love for the chase in many a young heart. These same hearts are grateful now in their disguise as old folks. They drew heavily on his recipe for a happy life.

The memory of his wit is a reflection of the good will he exuded to those around him. This is not to say he did not tease and chide. My father, Dinwiddie Lampton Jr., a young man who had just built his first horse van, was anxious to show his father-in-law, Mason, all his good work. After admiring the van for some period of time, Mason commented, "Dinwiddie, you are remarkable." With that, my father swelled with pride. The other shoe then dropped. "You have been able to put every mistake I have made on my vans over the last fifty years into this one van." My father's swelled chest quickly deflated after his chiding.

Mason's humor revealed itself in many forms. Often he prepared place cards for the evening dinners. On these he would write a rhyme about the guest. These were always fun and exciting to read. On one occasion he wrote to his son, Calvin, advice on how to handle his new bride.

> Now my son that you are old and able
> Take a seat at the head of the table
> Feel the edge of your carving knife
> Steal a glance at your charming wife
> And then when she speaks of a mistake you've made
> Then, my son, use the blade.

This ditty may have caused beautiful Josephine, Calvin's bride, to wonder what sort of family she had joined, but from other perspectives, the poem was a great bit of fun.

He was mischievous with all of his grandchildren. Tales of settlers coming down the Ohio, fighting Indians, and ghosts were the main fare of most bedtime stories. Hoofprints in the wood floors and bloodstains from when it served as a hospital after the Battle of Franklin, all helped populate the house with ghosts and ghouls. The wind would travel down the old chimneys, and the branches would scratch the windows. No one needed television. The master storyteller left terror in your heart with barely a few words uttered.

He was remorseless in his boyish pranks. At what we will call a "Big Boy Party"—a lovely seated affair with silver, crystal, and all the notable gentry of Nashville attending—he, in his effort to entertain me, a boy of eight, threw a firecracker under the seat of an imposing dowager who jumped no less than three feet in the air. We both ran from the room with my grandmother, Sara, screaming, "Mason. . . ."

I have asked my father what he would say in this foreword. He is now eighty-six and adores his critic of that long ago horse van. He said without question, "Mason's number one admonition was to 'avoid form without substance.'" This is the right message for all of us in this changing world. *Gone Away* expresses his love of the mystery of Nature. We must not allow pomposity to overshadow the joy of a dawn or the sound of a pack in full cry. These joys are lost on civilization as people become more severed from the countryside. In turn, we become more alienated from the city folk in our sport. We must entice them to understand our religion by sharing the fun. Mason Houghland understood this. To be with him was fun no matter what age you were. To be with him you were important no matter who you were. These are the lasting memories that I have lived with. They have provided a very real true north from which I have often taken direction.

Courage, diligence, levity, and wit were his tools. I hope you enjoy his book as he will entwine your heart with these same tools in this third printing of his *Gone Away*.

Mason H. Lampton, M.F.H.
Midland Fox Hounds

August 2000

FOREWORD

Fox-hunting is not merely a sport—and it is more nearly a passion than a game. It is a religion, a racial faith. In it are the elements that form the framework upon which beliefs are built: the attempt to escape from life as it is a life as we would have it; an abiding love of beauty; and an unconscious search for the eternal verities of fair play, loyalty and sympathetic accord, which are so clouded in our mundane existence.

It is a primitive faith, a "survival" the sociologist would term it, and harks back to the clear and simple outlook of our tribal gods. Through the years it goes on because, after the flush of many dawns, the thrill of never-ending pursuit, the sweet spice of danger, the simple tragedies of the field, and the weary darkness of long roads home, a few always become attuned to Nature's wondrous harmony of which they themselves are a part.

Like all religions it has many sects. There are the very "High Church" hunters with carefully observed ritual, who need form to guard the spirit and ceremonial to nourish belief. It is these Brahmans of the chase who make the picture the world sees, the scarlet coats on green fields, the great leaps, the beautiful backgrounds. They play a great part and merit the recognition of great effort. But in shadowy outline beyond them, outnumbering them a hundred to one, are legions of Fox-hunters, like Franciscan Brothers, whose profession of faith neither poverty nor sacrifice can dim, some who must even deny themselves the necessities in order to keep a couple of hounds.

On horseback, on muleback, or more often afoot, every night of the year, somewhere in every state in the Union, the horns of this great army of "hill-toppers" awaken the echoes of field and of forest.

MASON HOUGHLAND, M. F. H.

September 26, 1933.
  Green Pastures,
    Brentwood, Tennessee.

CONTENTS

		Page
Dedication		v
Foreword to the New Edition		vii
Foreword		xiii
List of Illustrations		xvii
Apology		xix

Chapter		
1	Introductory	1
2	Foxhunters	5
3	The Fox	9
4	Foxhounds	21
5	The Pack	45
6	Training	51
7	Breeding	61
8	Food	73
9	The Kennel	81
10	Hunting	85
11	Scent	111
12	The Whipper-In Alias The Whip	117
13	Horses	123
14	Landowners	129
15	Riding To Hounds	135
Epilogue		145

LIST OF ILLUSTRATIONS

	Page
Foxes will get a great laugh	iii
Look over menu	vi
All were hard hunters but Jim was one of the hardest	1
A little fire high on a far hill	5
Into that Fairy world to which they seem at times to have access	9
Just in time to see him kill a hen	13
His life is packed full of desperate adventure	21
Give him to a boy who lives up in the hills	38
The important thing about a pack is that it works as a unit	45
Flying Cloud turned so quickly that he rolled over and over	48
Biscuits are the trainers' trick	51
Five pups are enough for one bitch to rear	61
The test of feed is how the hound feels	73
Shade, water and drainage	81
Let them work the ground with care	85
A lone hound was reaching for his brush	100
A fox crossing a field leaves a track of scent oil	111
Shame them for their misbehaviour	117
Eight miles from home	123
Sons or grandsons of landowners	129
They drink the headiest drafts that man can quaff	135
Many fences must be led over	138
Mason Houghland, M. F. H., Painted by Goode Davis	144
Gone Away	Finale

APOLOGY

This is no brief in defense of foxhunting. The game is doubtless destined to go over the hills to oblivion along with wood fires, crossroad stores, steamboats, and croquet. And this "compendium of knowledge" is worthless for either the man who sits upon a stump at the top of a windswept hill with a hand cupped to his ear, or the stout broker upon two thousand dollars worth of horsehide who gallops behind hounds on Saturdays. In fact, I hardly know who should read this book, — for but few good foxhunters can or do read, and as this and subsequent pages will mutely evidence, fewer can write. But I think the foxes would get a great laugh over these sage observations about outwitting them. Maybe they can read, — they certainly can do everything else.

THE AUTHOR

All were hard hunters but Jim was one of the hardest.

CHAPTER I

INTRODUCTORY

You get close to the witchery of Nature when you try to read the story of a fox's journey. And upon a November dawn when the world lies still and the fog wraiths slip out of the embraces of the streams to hurry for the shelter of quiet shadowed woodlands, there is no ordered sequence of reason. The country is then a misty illusion, and a fox is neither in the world nor out of it, but seems to travel along the borderland and to step at will over on the Aesop side with the animals and the "Little People" who have escaped from man's horizon.

Of course, the oldest animal relationship upon earth is that of a man and a dog following quarry. So, when you and your hound follow a fox, you go back to the beginning, the dawn age when man's own animal cunning was first supplemented by the nose of his new found friend, the dog. And the unsolved mystery of a trail's end is an old, old problem not subject to laboratory analysis. My father's hounds were in the charge of a bearded African, who wore gold earrings and had the secrets of the Stone Age, direct and unfiltered by the written word. Sometimes at a confusing "loss," he would shake his grizzled head and announce, "That fox wasn't here no mo'h," in tones clearly indicating that the gods had intervened in the matter. Jehovah's interest in the welfare of the sparrow was known to me then, but old "Uncle Ike" convinced me that the fox came under another aegis and belonged upon the left side of the board with the dispossessed and the strange ones who dwelt in the shadows, and that when hard pressed might invoke the aid of his older kinsman, the Devil. Now, playing the Devil's game is frequently a stimulating pastime, and when B'rer Fox calls upon our Ancient Adversary to help him out, the chase becomes a riddle that needs luck to solve. In a way, running a fox is like playing cards with a magician—the game can be strictly orthodox for a long time but legerdemain may be employed in a crisis. Since no hunter wants to kill an able fox, the pursuit of one is really a game of tag, or "Prisoners' Base," rather than a hunt. And it is the last of the "Dawn" games, the preweapon contests between men and animals. The people who play would be classed by anthropologists, no doubt, as "primitives," for they set great store upon courage, speed, stamina and kindred attributes and leave the gainful pursuits to the Phoenicians.

Foxhunters share with farmers and with fishermen a distinctive and noble phase of life in that their gain is no man's loss. And for this or other reasons, the men, women and children who follow the sweet cry of hounds are a most satisfactory kind of people. They are not, I am afraid, brilliant. They constantly see their hounds (and themselves) outwitted by a fox and so, quite naturally, come to assume that the hounds have little sense. The sincerity of this conviction is well illustrated by an experience my friend Vernon Sharp had some years ago at the forks of Lick Creek. It was late and cold, and he had ridden far when he came to the store there. He hitched his horse and went in to buy some sausage. Back by the stove there was a chequer board resting upon a nail keg. At one side of it sat the storekeeper and across from him a long-eared "Pot-licker" hound. Neither paid any attention to the customer, but he gasped with astonishment to see that the man and the hound were actually deep in a game of chequers, and almost held his breath until it ended. But when it did, he told the storekeeper that the hound must be the smartest dog in the world.

"Pshaw," answered the storekeeper, very much annoyed, "he ain't smart —I don't lay claim to being a good chequer player but I beat him three out of four games myself."

Regardless, however, of what you may think of the intelligence of foxhunters or of hounds, neither of us will question the cunning of a fox, and the fascination of his pursuit has bred a distinct type of man. Foxhunters, like musicians, are born. You couldn't become one simply by practice. Doubtless, Nature produces them in some sort of balanced ratio, — based upon the number of foxes. Like antelope, they are not yet extinct but have been crowded back into remote places. Fortunately, most of them are born in quiet countrysides where there are rolling hills, clear streams, and occasional woodlands so matted with honeysuckle, wild roses, and briars that even in winter the foxes can safely lie in snug retreat. Sometimes these foxhunting babies are born in log houses up where the valley is narrow and the stream runs swiftly. Or, as often, the scene of their nativity is an old brick house, back from the pike, where mahogany and silver gleam in the firelight, but I never heard of one born in a house without a fireplace. This is a lucky caprice of Nature, for foxhunters must have a wood fire to sprawl before when they come in wet, tired, cold and content after a long day in the saddle. Perhaps the babies who are to become great hunters have a secret whispered in their ears by the Angels before they set out upon their journey; or, perhaps, they are sent only to beautiful mothers for whom the world smiles. In any event, foxhunters are generally happy fellows, who find life a pleasant thing. One reason for this is that their sport is elastic and fits any purse.

"A poor man can keep a foxhound," observed Bill Nye, "and some are so poor that they keep four or five." But, as my grandfather once remarked to grandmother, "Even a large pack is less of a purse drain than being the principal contributor to a country church!"

The term "foxhunter" is a Catholic one and indicates an attitude towards life, rather than a standardized participation in a sport, for some gallop after hounds, some have only "shanks pony," and others sit on a hilltop and listen. A writer in the "Chase Magazine," describing some hunting companions at a night hunt said: "All were hard hunters, but Jim was one of the hardest I have seen. Time after time during the night he would arouse himself, throw back his blanket, leave the fire, go to the edge of the woods—and *listen*." By contrast, I once knew a lad by the name of Stanley Murray who had schooled himself to *run* with hounds and did an amazing job of it, vaulting over fences and going like blazes at times.

"GONE AWAY!"

The proportion of people that hunt is quite small and, perhaps, growing smaller. Horses and hounds may even become outmoded. During the first World War, we had little use for cavalry yet its accoutrements still carried about them the faint aura of old respectability. It was customary to see air pilots in boots and spurs. No one saw the brave young eaglets of this conflict in such borrowed plumage. Those of us who started life in the pre-motor age still have a feeling that there is a touch of "class" about a horse and hound, but younger and mayhap less sinful people give this combination the uplifted eyebrow that generally greets cockfighting. Perhaps in Virginia, Kentucky, in the remote valleys of Tennessee, or in the rolling isolation of northern Mississippi, the ancient sport will be respectable for another half century, but already in many areas the only place you will find foxhunters is —gathering dust in the family album. But what a wonderful group they are and have been, — the flat bellied fraternity who meet at dawn with the wild red fox and whose tired horses stumble at night into darkened stable doors. They have all the fun, these gallant lads and lassies who follow where the hounds lead. The mad wild cry of hounds has set their blood afire and they have flown over the gates, rattled the rails, and drunk the very wine of life, — so need no tears.

A little fire high on a far hill.

CHAPTER II

FOXHUNTERS

When we say foxhunting we mean a game played with horses, as well as hounds, but to more men, however, foxhunting now means a little fire high on a far hill, the melody of hounds' voices rising, falling, dying away throughout the night, and the flush of triumph as their own favorite's voice is heard at times in front. And these men know hound pedigrees, starting with the couple Nimrod bought from Noah. If a great stallion hound is developed somewhere, bitches are sent to him from hamlets so remote that it is a day's journey out to a hard road. Such hunters love their hounds and believe in their stamina, speed, and prowess. Their "fox races" are social affairs that offer hound owners an opportunity to escape into the campfire scene, which is so essential to the happiness of men.

One night in the early Spring, years ago, a group of us had met for such a hunt near Versailles, Kentucky and, shortly after hounds were cast, noticed a lantern far away across the valley bobbing along toward us. Each time a hound spoke the lantern bearer evidently stopped but presently turned and the light gradually was lost to view.

"Who was that with the light?" Len Shouse asked.

"Why, that's Will," answered Sam Wooldridge. "He's on his way to see his girl. Has gone to see her every Wednesday night for ten years."

About midnight the lantern bobbed into sight again, but this time dipped down the far hill, across the valley, and presently the man who carried it walked into our fire's light. After the usual exchange of greetings, which included pulling the cob from the mouth of a jug and some long gurgling sounds, the traveler blew out his lantern and sat down.

"Will," queried Sam, "you been going to see that girl once a week for ten years. Why don't you marry her?"

"Well, it's like this, Mr. Wooldridge," came the slow and reflective answer. "She says that I'm too poor to keep four hounds and a wife but that she will marry me if I will give up two hounds. But I ain't never bin able to decide which two hounds to give up."

I heard Will's hounds run one night afterwards, and they really were good ones. But I have never gotten a look at his girl so can venture no opinion upon his dilemma. However, perhaps she is happier waiting for the lantern's gleam than in being a foxhunter's wife, for those ladies evidently are at times lonesome. One in some anger addressed the following letter to a foxhunters' magazine:

"Dear Editor:

My husband is a foxhunter. Every Saturday night when I want to go to town, he takes his hounds and goes to the woods. We have been married seven years. I used to be thought right good looking in this neighborhood. I have been asked out to box suppers. If he doesn't change his ways, I might change mine.

Yours truly,

A Foxhunter's Widow"

Surely, every foxhunter who had been married seven years and read that letter must have had food for thought!

Night foxhunting is, to a large degree, hound racing. A night hunter wants a fast hound, but more than anything else, he demands one that will "stay," for when his hound gives up and comes to the fire, he is subject to the same merciless taunts that greet a chicken fighter when his game cock is more discreet than valorous. Gameness is the one absolute requirement of the sport. Other faults may be obscured at times by night, but lack of courage and stamina rarely is so hidden.

It sometimes happens that a night hunter becomes so absorbed in fox chasing that he takes his hand from the plough and his person from the hearth for longer periods than are, perhaps, conducive to good husbandry. Upon the occasion of a hunt at Dawson Springs, Kentucky, many hunters were stopping at the principal resort hotel which had a bathroom upon both floors, served the soup before the meat and was, therefore, luxurious. Among the group who wassailed and celebrated was a small homespun hunter from the forks of the creek over in a neighboring county. With a cowhorn always over his shoulder and a glass in his hand, he terminated the day's sport with joyful celebrations.

"Jake," observed one serious hunter, "how can you carry on this way? Your poor wife and children are alone in that cabin and here you are living like a king!"

"Pshaw!" answered Jake, "my wife ain't got a thing in the world to worry about. I ain't going to be gone but a week and I left her with a side of bacon and a sack of cornmeal."

It was Jake's Socratic decision for the Cemetery Board that made him forever famous. The Board was meeting at the courthouse one day trying to decide what kind of a fence to build around the graveyard. The four members were divided, and deadlocked when our friend, Jake, passed, leading a couple of hounds by one hand and carrying a jug in the other.

"Suppose we let Jake decide the question about the fence," was the happy suggestion of the Chairman, to which the other Board members readily agreed. So, Jake was called in and the situation explained. A board fence would cost less, but an iron fence had more dignity.

"Well," said Jake, scratching his head, "since you asked me, I'm bound to tell you folks what I think, and that's this—them that's out don't want in, and them that's in thar cain't git out, — so two strands of smooth wire had orght to be sufficient."

What a shame it is that two strands of smooth wire are not deemed "sufficient" everywhere, instead of the barricades of woven and barbed wire that make a "no-man's land" out of the fairest countryside. But since it is that way and vast areas are almost impossible to ride over, the future apparently belongs to the night hunter, for he can carry on when the man on horseback is helpless.

The outstanding difference between the night hunter and the foxhunter that follows his hounds is that the former in reality is racing hounds one against the other, while the latter is running a pack of hounds in competition with a fox. The night hunter speaks with pride of the fox that runs ten and twelve hours, whereas the day hunter blushes if his pack takes a third of that time to drive a fox to ground. Nothing so well illustrates the value of teamwork as this, for the night hunter has much the better individual hounds. But, his hounds are apt to be jealous of strange competitors and to run first to beat their fellow and second to catch the fox. Sometimes it seems as though the mission of the fox was to lay a drag or to work a course for the contestants to follow. Many of us have a bad auditory recording system and must *see* hounds run rather than hear them, but for the fellows whose ears are accurate, night hunting provides one of the fairest and cleanest of all sports and it attracts only men of friendly hearts and real character. In fact, there probably is no such group of men in any fraternal organization as that which is so faithful in attendance at the Hunters' Lodge.

Into that Fairy world to which they seem at times to have access.

CHAPTER III

THE FOX

The red fox is one of the most beautiful animals in the world. In motion he writes a poem of movement. People who have never seen one gasp with awe and delight when first they view this brave marauder. In color he varies from dark "red" to lemon, with feet, lower legs and eartips of black. The brush is often of a slightly darker shade than the body and may, or may not be, tipped with white. When he walks, each hindfoot "tracks" with the forefoot on the same side. His stride is between fourteen and seventeen inches. When running, the hindfeet come down back of the forefeet. Most fast animals, including the horse, overreach with their hindfeet when at speed, but the fox does not. In soft ground, the whole foot is imprinted, heels, toes and claws. When he is running, the toe marks are spread. He has four claws on his hindfeet and, counting the dew claw, five on his forefeet.

His brush is carried straight, not ever curled, and always raised at an angle. When, if ever, he lowers it, the curtain is coming down upon the brave drama of his life. On coming down a steep hill, the brush is over his back; when turning suddenly at speed, he swings it sideways to balance himself. In cold weather, when sleeping, he uses it for a muff.

Although the fox is scientifically identified as a member of the dog family, it has never so far as is known crossed with a dog. Foxes generally mate in January and whelp in March. The fox cubs do not open their eyes for nearly three weeks, nor make such use of their legs for about six weeks. The dog fox helps the vixen to feed the cubs and brings them field mice, rabbits, etc., which he has killed. When the cub is seven or eight months old, he knows a certain amount of territory and can easily kill the food he needs. As he grows older, he travels further and gains new ideas about how to take care of himself in a curious world of cur dogs, men and traps. By the time he is about two years old, he finds that he has no valid title to the property he occupies and must either dispossess the resident dog fox or "homestead" somewhere for himself. For a fox has a territory of his own and he lives off of it as a man does off a farm, rarely leaving except to court a widow or to escape the tax collectors. Few animals are much wilder than a fox, and yet he survives even a suburban development of his territory.

What does a fox eat? According to shooting men, his diet includes many quail. I, personally, do not believe the fox to be included among the important enemies of this bird. Some years ago, I purchased a tract of land near Cross Plains, Tennessee, because it had more foxes in residence than any place I knew. A year later, the Middle Tennessee Bird Dog Association persuaded me to let them use it as a permanent Field Trial ground because it had (and has) more quail than any place in the region. The reason a fox doesn't eat many quail is simply because they are so hard to get. A fox's nose is certainly no better than that of a good bird dog, nor is he a specialist on this one bird. Twice in my life I have seen a fox stalking quail. Each time he gave up the job. And, it was obvious that too much time and trouble were involved to make it a profitable occupation for him.

A fox is the greatest killer of rats and field mice of any known animal. He eats myriads of beetles, grasshoppers, and other insects. Blackberries are his favorite dessert. He hunts mostly by scent and has a nose that tells him the whole story of what is going on, but he uses his eyes much better than a dog does and little that moves escapes his notice. Like a great many human beings, the fox prefers night life to the day. Scent is then better, and also neighbors have less opportunity to meddle. However, he is very frequently abroad in the day and in addition may either get home late in the morning or start out early in the afternoon for a hunt. The adult does not lie much in holes and uses them more for a refuge than an apartment. He has his regular travel ways and, when run by hounds, is likely, as all foxhunters know, to traverse his established "crossings." It is surprising how little space is required to give him shelter. In a rocky country, the ledges afford him splendid protection from rain, sleet and snow. In a woodland country, a hollow log or a leaning tree offer him luxurious accommodations, but he is satisfied with almost insignificant shelter. When the sun is bright, a broomsedge field provides ideal seclusion for sun bathing and is a favorite place for him to lie. He likes best to lie in cover of considerable size, which combines some opportunity to view the country. So, a wooded hill or a cliff is his choice for normal residence.

Although the most alert and wary of animals, the fox at times will, after a big meal, stretch out in the sun and sleep "like a drunken sailor." I, once, in Warren County, Kentucky, came upon one in a thin clump of woods lying upon a rock in a sleep so profound that he never heard me until I could almost touch him. The picture of that beautiful red fox, spotlighted by sunshine, sound asleep in a beech forest upon a white limestone rock, was one that will long lighten days for me.

In his own hunting country, a fox is at home and knows its intimate details down to every rock and stick. But if hounds push him beyond home boundaries, he is far less able to handle the situation. Then he passes by many a good refuge, and depends upon speed to save him until he can make a turn and get back to his own territory. This is why January frequently gives long, straight runs. A fox goes courting, and when hounds strike his line, he may be miles from home. So, he immediately starts for familiar country and wastes no time in going.

We are all inclined to forget that a fox's view of the country is very different from our own. He sees the world from so slight an elevation that even grass and weeds may block his vision. You sit on your horse and watch a hunted fox cross a field, and wonder why he doesn't see the shepherd dog on the other side. The marvel is that he becomes aware of the enemy as soon as he does, when you consider that he has so limited a field of vision.

A fox has his regular "crossings" and generally uses them either when looking over his plantation, or when fleeing from hounds. Observant hunters get to know these runways almost to the foot. The first time I ever went foxhunting I was taken by the old negro, "Uncle Ike," who took care of hounds for my father. He put me "on a crossing" and since I was very small, I soon tired, climbed off my pony and laid down on the ground. Subsequently, both the fox and the hounds ran over me. Uncle Ike was very clear about the fox crossings, as are most old hunters. Br'er Fox will vary his course if hard pressed or to take advantage of a favorable wind, but like the Mississippian who finally went to work, does so "with the greatest reluctance."

If you stop and think about the matter, the fox view of it is the only practical one. He is disturbed by hounds. Why should he run off helter skelter like a rabbit? To begin with, he isn't frightened so he takes time to plan the route of escape. Secondly, experience has taught him that while there are several possible routes, there is a first choice, — so he takes it. But he is not foolish about the matter, for he will change plans at an instant's notice. The one thing to always bear in mind about a fox is that he is actually smart. And he doesn't get drunk nor use tobacco, so his head is frequently clearer than is that of the Captains who pursue him. And he will always do the wise thing. Nine times out of ten, the course he chooses will be so sensible that even smart people, like you and me, are unable to anticipate it.

What a fellow this Red Ranger is! How well he meets his problems! The question of food is simple. In an area like Middle Tennessee where the land is rich, the climate mild, and the people too kindly to shoot him, he can solve his food problems in a fifth the time a man can. Like man, he devotes a good deal of time to courtship, and the full light of a winter moon plays havoc with his emotions, but he still has the bigger portion of his hours free all the year. Think that over, and remember the people you see who work hard from sun-up to sunset for groceries and a roof. Who then is smarter, a fox or a man? He arranges shelter, food, security, romance and a home with no great effort. How many times have you ever seen a poor, crippled or sick fox? Perhaps when their span of life is done, they slip directly across the border into that Fairy world to which they seem at times to have access. I'm sure they come near "dissolving into thin air" upon occasions, and it may be that they have remembered how to manage even that "crossing."

THE HUNTED FOX

When you have been pursuing foxes for forty years and have come at last to the conclusion that you should write a book upon how to carry on the Chase, it is humiliating to have to confess that you can indicate no rules that will insure the capture of one fox. The truth of the matter is that if a red fox gets a fair break, he will outwit us and our hounds everytime we chase him. When the National Fox Hunters Association held its first meet at Florence, Alabama, the 300 best hounds in America were, without notice, cast upon a peninsula where the fox was denied escape upon three sides by

Just in time to see him kill a hen.

water and upon the other side almost shut off by a crowd of people strung out like skirmishers across the neck of the land. The fox did not only escape with ease, but so ran that not many people even viewed him.

A hunted fox rarely travels faster than is necessary to keep ahead of the hounds. The picture of a frightened fox, terrified by the pursuit and running at top speed all the way, is generally an imaginary one. On a moderate scenting day, a fox is not even annoyed by the brave lads who sniff at his track and bawl threats behind him. I recall very well upon one occasion hounds ran a fox through the negro village of Brentwood. It seemed to me that they would catch him when he got on the pike. I galloped fast down "Hard Scuffle Lane" and came out on the Wilson Pike just in time to see him kill a hen, pick her up and trot unconcernedly across the railway. Two hundred yards behind him, the cry of the pack roared like Niagara Falls. Fear is simply not part of a fox's makeup. He thinks as clearly in "the jaws of death" as he does at any other time.

About a year ago we were running a hard-driven grey fox that finally took refuge in a small leaning tree. When we rode up, he lay in the tree's crotch just above the reach of forty hounds that, crazed with excitement, vainly times without number, leaped upwards at him. My friend, John Sloan, climbed the tree. The fox shifted his eyes, watched Sloan and the hounds with calm impartiality, and just at the right moment leaped into that mass of tongue and tooth beneath him. It looked like hara-kiri in earnest. But far from it! The fox had watched until he saw an opening, then leaped, twisted, turned, and was safe behind the goal posts of his own den before the confused hounds had quit biting each other.

When a fox is found and goes away, he generally seems to have pretty clearly in mind what to do. Usually he runs a route that has proven to be a useful one upon previous occasions of that kind. If it happens to be an excellent scenting day, he may be forced to abandon his "regular run" and make for a distant hill or some large woodland that offers refuge. And if hard enough pressed, he may after a few turns be forced to clear out of his own estate and into unfamiliar territory. But ninety-nine times out of a hundred, he manages to work his way back to his own district.

You cannot but conclude that a fox enjoys the Chase. Of course, if he were frequently in danger of his life, he wouldn't. Natural instinct for survival would see that he removed himself permanently from the vicinity of the hounds. I am embarrassed to say that there are two red fox dens within a half mile of our kennels. Every now and then at night, a fox will come up near the kennels and bark in an impudent and provocative fashion. Years ago, we kenneled a pack of hounds at the "Lost River" near Bowling Green, Kentucky. There was a fox den one hundred yards away when we built the kennel, and for aught I know foxes are still using it. It was a regular nightly occurrence for one of our fox neighbors to come up close to the kennel and bark. I am sure he said unpleasant things in canine language, for each time hounds grew choleric with rage.

Much of the principal foxhunting territory of America has a limestone base and is full of holes. Yet, many foxes frequently disdain to go in no matter how many hounds are out, nor how hard they are driven.

When hounds lose a fox, he quite often leisurely doubles back to the cover where he was found. Sometimes I have thought that he and the hounds not only made a game of it but had rules something akin to those of "Prisoner's Base" that we all played in childhood. Maybe the fox is supposed to come back and touch home base each time. Certainly some sanctuary is recognized. Once when we were hunting in Mr. Lem Motlow's country, hounds ran a fox hard for an hour or more and he finally took refuge upon a rocky ledge which crossed the face of a small cliff. Two hounds got out upon the ledge but made no effort to molest him, and fox and hounds stood there in perfect amity looking down at the riders as though to say, "Well, the game is over. What shall we play now?"

The ordinary gait of a fox is a canter, and no other animal moves with such effortless precision. Even at a run, he normally appears to glide along in an easy movement. I have yet to see the hound that could tie a full-grown dog fox in a short burst of speed. A tired fox holds his head low and lowers his brush slightly. I can recall seeing but two or three dead beat foxes that appeared to have been dragging their brush. A hard run fox will sometimes manage to get a fresh one to take his turn. Whether this is accident or design, it is difficult to prove, but it frequently has the outward appearance of a managed job. A hunted fox will sometimes go to a hole, stop, decline to go in, double back on his line, and go on his way. It is a very confusing maneuver, both to a hound and to a foxhunter.

Once in his own country, Wooldridge took me to watch a fox trick hounds. The cry was a mile away. We tied our horses and lay down in the edge of a sedge grass field facing a pasture, bordered on the right by an old stone wall. The fox presently ran right by us into the pasture and then executed the most amazing maneuver. Unhurried, he doubled up in his line, then made a circle of about a hundred yards in diameter which closed near the wall. Then he jumped on the wall, ran backwards a few yards, gave a great leap off on the other side, and ran off at right angles to his original course. It could only have been a premeditated move to confuse hounds. And yet, many writers insist that a fox does not realize he is pursued by scent! Three minutes later, the pack was abreast of us with "Big Stride" in a short lead. Without a check, he ran the circle just as the fox had traced it and reared upon the wall sniffing for the scent. At that instance, Ch. "Cleo" leaped to the top of the wall, cried the line along it, and leaped off where the fox had jumped. In a flash, that great pack, which included six National Champions, had honored her and were over and away in full cry. But even though they may have been the best hounds of their day, they never caught that fox and never will. Doubtless, in some wilderness Valhalla where the mead flows like moonshine and the echo of horn and hound forever trembles in the air, they are still racing to solve that ancient dispute.

The red fox swims well and shows no fear of water. I think that he almost knows its usefulness in confusing hounds. At least, I never saw him traveling in a stream bed except when chased. Time and time again, however, he travels in the bed of a shallow "branch" when hounds are on his trail. And a very useful trick it is. Only a veteran hound solves it. The trick has many variations and all naturally confuse hounds. Frequently, the fox leaves the water at a certain spot which he has found to be useful in halting the noisy ruffians who follow. It may be a down-tree with a branch in the water or a patch of oak leaves in a little cove, or a sticky mud bank, but whatever place he makes use of he seems to have thought about in advance.

In 1937, Major W. B. Scott, M. F. H. of the North Cotswold Hounds in Gloucestershire, sent me a young bitch called "Startle." The day she arrived after an uninterrupted trip of 3,500 miles, I was going hunting and took her along to give her some exercise. It wasn't a good scenting day to start with and hounds lost almost as soon as they left the cover. She cried the line presently, the pack harked to her and were soon running hard. A mile and a half further on in a big wheatfield scent suddenly vanished. It was the old Indian rope trick, — the fox seemed to have climbed into thin air; hounds circled in vain, the line just ended. Then I saw "Startle" double back up a little rivulet, head down and hackles up. She waded a hundred yards, stepped out and cried the fox. He had run out into the wheatfield, then dropped into the rivulet, and doubled right back in the water, practically in the face of the hounds. Like many things a hunted fox does, this seemed a well thought out stratagem to bother hounds.

Another ruse which foxes employ is to run the top of a rail fence. It is possible that a fox runs the top of a wall without thought as to its effect upon his scent track, for he uses walls to some degree on his own hunts. But the top rail of a worm fence is little more convenient than a tight rope, even to a fox. And when he runs one, he must do so for the sole purpose of confusing hounds. Not long ago, down in the famous "Lick Creek Country," which is still all worm rail fences, a number of us had front row seats at a perfect demonstration of the fence trick. Hounds had been driving a fox for some time and had at last gotten up close to him. Riders could easily view the Red Ranger, and only the dead weeds and grasses kept the hounds from enjoying a "sight chase." As he neared the bottom of a field, the fox sighted a rail fence and leaped upon it. Four or five seconds later, the hounds were at the fence. The fox trotted along the top rail and the hounds, head down, slowly cried the line along the fence below his. Not a hound looked up. Three feet above them was his majesty in plain view and in, at least momentarily, safety. When he came to a cross fence, he ran out upon it a little ways to a thicket and dropped off, headed in a new direction.

Foxes that have been frequently hunted generally slip out of their home covers long in advance of the arrival of hounds. Care must be used in approaching these veterans. If wind or terrain don't interfere, hounds should be cast upon the side of the wood opposite from where you want the fox to run. For example, if upon one side the wood strings out into a brushy ravine along which the fox can steal away unobserved and upon another side is a big blue grass pasture, your choice is easy. You draw through the ravine and try to force the fox out into the open. And with a friend who understands his job posted along the flank, you may sometimes help to persuade the fox to give you a gallop across the open.

A dead beat fox will go in anywhere. He is smart enough to know that no new risk offers the certain danger that the approaching pack does, and so flees into whatever sanctuary presents itself. Some years ago, a fox we were chasing, rushed and harried by the bawling bullies that drove him out of his home territory, ran straight into a negro cabin by the roadside. Mammy and seven or eight pickaninnies were inside, but Br'er Fox paid them no mind. Under the bed he went. Negro women in the country have their full share of cunning, and this one immediately slammed the door in the face of the lead hound. Her instinctive action rang down the curtain upon what would have been the only rousing third act I might have ever seen. Seven negroes, forty hounds, and a fox in a fourteen by fourteen room should have provided song and story for years to come. Even as it was, the scene was spirited enough; forty hounds, baying and slobbering at the door and windows, negroes crying, praying and pleading inside. What happened to the fox I never knew, for in all these years I have never again invaded those remote hills. Perhaps he stayed on with his new friends and lies smugly by their fire upon winter nights, recalling now and then the great day when they "fooled the white folks."

When a fox is found early in the morning, he won't run as well as he will after noon because his stomach will be full. The earlier the fuller is the rule. Sometimes a hunted fox stops and rolls in manure or carrion. This quite effectively confuses foxhounds. However, hounds will often do the same thing. So, it is doubtless a luxury and not a stratagem.

While a fox seems to adjust his pace to that of his pursuers, this does not mean that he stops when they do. On the contrary, he continues to slip through the country and puts an increasingly long distance between himself and the hounds at each check. Now and again under pressure, the fox turns into a strong wind, but he prefers running with it. I think he has learned that hounds come towards him faster when he turns into the wind. After all, he is more frequently a pursuer than pursued and he stalks his game by scent even though he rarely runs it. So, he must understand what difference "up" and "down" wind make to the pursuer.

When a hard-driven fox has decided to "go in," it is very difficult to turn him from his hole. Upon one occasion up in Robertson County when a fox kept trying to go in, a girl asked permission to take on the task of turning him back from his hole. The first time she waved her stick and turned him, but the next time, harder pressed, he bared his teeth and much to her dismay jumped over her shoulder. However men as well have been intimidated by a homeward bound fox.

A fox is very fast and can easily beat the fleetest hound in a short burst of speed. Uphill or in a rough country, the hound is no match for him. In open country over smooth going, a swift hound can overtake a fox. Over a distance of ground and for a short while, a thoroughbred horse can move faster than either of them. In an open sod country and upon a good scenting day, a fox is certain to be hard pressed by a good pack of hounds. But, there are few such countries and fewer good packs of hounds, so our fox friends have us beaten.

A hard pressed fox does not look back when hounds get near him. What a wonderful lot of cool headedness this indicates. A man who is being pursued is forever looking backwards. Most of us normally look backward more frequently than we do forward. Not so the fox! The mistakes he has made join "yesterday's seven thousand years" the instant they are made. What concerns him is the route ahead, — and so he makes few mistakes. You will rarely in a whole lifetime see a fox hemmed in or shut off from a route of escape. How different from us and from all other animals!

Smarter than a man, faster than a hound, and braver than a lion—that's a fox!

Foxes for restocking may always be bought at a moderate price from the Northern dealers who advertise in "The Chase" and other magazines. The best time to stock a country with young foxes is during the months of June and July. Then, the imported cubs have some size and strength, vegetation is thick and offers easy concealment, and food is plentiful. Put the foxes out in well-concealed holes near a stream or a spring and leave them a couple of days' supply of the kind of food they have been eating. Then for the next month, return two or three times a week and leave food. By Fall, they will be able to shift for themselves. Just before you release the cubs, strike them with a keen switch and frighten them. Many a young fox that has been reared in captivity is slow to hide from an approaching man and, so loses his life before he has learned the ways of the world.

It is an easy and inexpensive matter to keep a country stocked with foxes if you are not bothered by trappers. If you are, it is sometimes possible to provide these gentry with opportunities in town, or in some other part of the Nation. The worst one that ever bothered me was delighted to accept a loan for railway tickets to Detroit. Since he has made no return, either of money or of person, he must be happier, . . . and I am. In the North, and in a very few of the poorer hill regions of the South, there are people who will shoot foxes. But such depravity is born of either ignorance or poverty and will, we hope, some day vanish with both. In at least one State, Tennessee, the old law of Vulpicide holds on, and while the man who kills a red fox does not hang, he meets punishment as serious as if he had "lead poisoned" a neighbor. In parts of West Virginia the red fox is protected, and similar laws exist in other states.

His life is packed full of desperate adventure.

CHAPTER IV

THE FOXHOUND

A foxhound is a warrior. His life is packed full of desperate adventure, high speed, the tumult of camp, the roar of battle, — and swift oblivion. The omnipresent horror of wire, the cruelty of traps, threaten his every step. He lives and dies, "not for the lust of killing" but consecrated to one great purpose, — the Chase. The qualities he needs are nose, drive, stamina, tongue, speed and "fox sense." He has been bred for a century and a half in this country for these qualities alone, and his conformation and appearance have been really incidental.

Up until the time of "Tennessee Lead" the qualities most frequently sought for were nose and cry, — hounds that could take the night line of a fox and in tones like a church bell announce each yard of the route from then on. For the century of this type of breeding, we have much to be grateful. It made possible the production of the faster hound which followed, and this great reservoir of nose and cry continues to make possible the experiments in breeding which, in the last century, have been worth so much. Hounds must depend upon their noses to run a fox. Really, all the talk about bone, straight legs, etc. is like judging a violinist by his appearance. We think of the bloodhound as having a wonderful nose because, by creeping along at a snail's pace and sniffing under a plaintain leaf, he can follow a cold trail. The foxhound snatches his evidence of the line at speed, and that requires a far better nose. Joe Thomas, in his great book "Hounds and Hunting," drives home the indisputable fact that "a hound is no faster than his nose." This is the one thing a foxhunter needs to be clear on if he wants to see his pack push a fox. And this doesn't mean three or four good noses in a pack, it means that every hound in it have a superior nose. The better the nose, the faster the hound, and the closer he will stay on the fox. This, of course, means "hotter" scent, shorter checks, and fewer losses. If you want to "roll the tambourine" and to push the Red Ranger across the country with some dash, think first of nose, *then* of drive and speed, for the fox is followed by scent alone.

"How," you may ask, "am I to be sure of the nose of a stallion hound owned by someone else?" You may well ask the question, for it propounds one of the most difficult problems connected with the development of a pack. Field trials offer one, and unless you have time to travel and hunt with many hounds, inquiry must solve the problem. To make successful inquiry, you must have many friends and acquaintances who know hounds. Of course, there may be a hound to suit you in your own or an adjoining country, and then you can have your own verification of his scenting powers. This is much better, for most foxhunters, and almost all night hunters, finally evaluate a hound not upon nose but upon speed. The friendly curtain of darkness lends reputation to some hounds that are not always faithful to the line.

When the National was first held at Florence, Alabama, upon the starting day of the Futurity a couple of hundred of America's best young hounds were entered. And they were no sooner cast than they had a big "Red" on his feet. The challenge of the pack must have induced him to see if the world was really round, for he fled across the cotton fields in the manner of a traveler bent upon outrunning the "Dixie Flyer." Hounds went away well packed and their cry split the sharp November air with a roar that set the countryside into action for miles around. Away went the riders upon mules, racking-horses and thoroughbreds, — galloping like the Furies and all drunk with the wine of the Chase. Straight as an arrow went the fox across the fields, through woods, up hill and down, pointed for the river and a sheltering bluff. And then at a bare cornfield, the hounds suddenly slowed down to a walk, the cry stopped, their heads went down in vain efforts to recover the pungent scent, and the glorious burst became a fruitless search. Some tried back, many ahead, and others circled, but not a hound spoke. Finally they gave it up. It was a real loss. But one saddle-backed, tri-colored hound slowly worked his way across the fallow ground. He wasn't saying anything, but his stern was flying and his head was down. For half a mile he pushed on and then in the edge of a sedge grass field ahead he cried once, then again. This last time, it was the triumphant challenge of a conqueror;

"I have it boys, — catch me if you can," he roared and was away. One hound out of two hundred whose nose said, "This is the way he went." The pack surged to him and we were off again "on the Glory Road." The hound was "Longstreet," a son of Sam Wooldridge's "Buzzard Wings," out of Eugene Torbett's great bitch, "Crooked Lena." Some months later, he came to head the Hillsboro Pack, which now includes some twenty couple of his progeny.

If you are starting a pack of hounds today, visit field trials in search of really good bitches. Be careful that those selected have been highly scored. Then pay the price the owners ask, provided hounds are shipped upon a month's trial basis. Hunt the bitches all you can, and decide first about their noses. Don't be misled about this quality under very favorable conditions versus bad conditions. Any hound seems to have a good nose when the ground is five degrees warmer than the air. Hunt the bitches in open country and follow them as closely as you can. If you can select four bitches with really good noses, you may lay the foundation for a pack. At least, you will have taken the right first step.

Since the sine qua non of a foxhound is Nose, this one essential quality should be the primary base of your selection for breeding. To puzzle out a cold line, most "pot lickers" serve well enough. But to get forward with it, to unravel the tangle, to ignore its inconsequential details, to interpret the true course from swiftly gleaned evidence, and to put the fox to running before he has had time to steal away on a long lead, takes bloodlines of the highest quality.

When your hound keeps returning to the last place where he found the scent and bawling out confirmation of the matter, he is a "dweller," and should be hastily disbarred. The hound with a real nose has confidence in his own ability to identify scent when he finds it, and wastes no time in confirming previously accepted evidence. The useful hound is the one that gets forward on the line. When you see a hound afraid to leave the vicinity where he lost the scent, you may know that he will never push a fox, unless by accident. Your fox-driving hound is perfectly aware that "he who hesitates is lost," that the fox is getting further and further away every second. So at a loss, he circles at speed, or, if a seasoned veteran, conducts a hasty sniffing inquiry at the places where he could have crossed had he been the fox.

When a fox is up and conditions are favorable, any hound can do a fair job of running. But when the day is unfavorable and scent is failing, it takes hounds of great nose to keep forward, even on a running fox. Watch such hounds when scent starts to fail. They press to stay with it and, at a definite loss, first cast forward at speed striving to pick the line up on a short arc ahead, rather than to puzzle out the intervening distance. Then failing to strike it off, they complete a wide circle, still at speed, intent upon picking up a sharp change of direction with as little loss in time as possible.

This illustration refers to the scent of a running fox and is not intended to imply that a good hound never slows down to work out a line. Rather, he goes as fast as the scent permits, — as long as he has a line. Then at a check, to make a successful quick cast, he must have a good enough nose to pick up the line at speed. Never allow yourself to be lured into breeding to a stallion hound because of his shape, carriage or speed, unless sure that the animal has a great nose. The only way to be sure is to watch him in competition and to see how he handles his fox. A hound may be as symmetrical as Apollo and as fast as Man O' War, but not valuable in a pack unless his nose is good. Bench shows are a dangerous influence. They cause breeders to overstress conformation. Happily they are associated with field trials, and performance outweighs everything else with real hunting men. But the influence of the bench show may yet ruin our hounds. We must remember that a foxhound is not a unit of livestock to be judged by bone and backline. He is a singer, an artist, a swordsman, — and like these is to be judged only upon performance.

SPEED

Physical speed perhaps is not entitled to the prominence we give it in our conversation, since its value is dependent first upon Nose, and then upon Courage and Stamina. If, however, you are determined to have a Pack that does the best possible job of running a fox, it is essential that all the hounds in it are nearly equal in speed. Failure to recognize this need is the most common mistake foxhunters make.

Even though you keep fifty hounds, if some are fast and some slow, you haven't a *Pack*. A Pack of hounds must run *together* if you are to have frequent good sport and infrequent losses. Even if such a Pack is a little slow, it will give you better sport than one unbalanced by a few extremely fast individuals.

However, the attitude of the hunters I know towards speed reminds me of the attitude of a young school teacher in our valley, years ago, toward a girl. He was serious minded, and had been too busy thinking about Homer to see Helen. Then, a girl came to visit at the house where he was boarding. Her hair was ash blond, her eyes big, startled, and a misty blue grey. As for her conformation, — *well,* whoever designed her intended trouble. But she lisped, only knew a few words, and wasn't sure in her numbers beyond ten. She turned the headlights once on the school teacher, and he couldn't see afterwards which way he was going. But, he ran around telling everybody about what a wonderful *mind* little Jezebel had! All hunters are, by speed in hounds, like men are about beauty in women. It is the number one quality in their minds. It causes a lot of bothers, but they excuse a hound most weaknesses if he can get out in front and stay there a while.

There is perhaps something in the sun's rays upon this continent that stimulates the desire for fast motion. Or it may be the great distances we travel that impels many of us to be constantly in a hurry. Everyone feels this cyclonic pressure. When my friend, Bill Scott, sent me the North Cotswold "refugee pack" at the outbreak of the war, unloading them on the dock in New York was no small problem. Without the help of Joe Thomas and his old huntsman, Charlie Carver, we would have had hounds scattered among the lambs down Wall Street way. On duty at the dock was a young Irish policeman, resplendent in blue broadcloth. He gave us a lot of help in a directive way, and as we finished loading in the Vicmead's hound van, said with a profound sigh,

"It makes me homesick for County Limerick to see the hounds again! How I wish I were back on the ould sod!"

Joe Thomas remarked that he seemed to be doing well and asked what in the world he could find fault with on these shores. The Hibernian looked down at his new shoes and twirled his stick with obvious pride. Then with a twinkle in his eyes, he replied,

"The only thing that bothers me in this country is these damned *clocks*."

I immediately wrung his hand. If he had also damned the wire, I would have embraced him. It is the clocks that put the pressure on us. When foxhunters went by sun-time doubtless there was less reason to push a fox so fast. However it be, I personally have never known anyone who didn't want a fast pack; although in this world of wire, about all one sees of such a pack is a blur across a clearing, silhouettes on a ridge, or some black, white and tan streaks across a meadow. A slower pack would doubtless provide much more entertainment if it were good. However, I shall keep on trying to breed fast ones, and so will you. Our grandfathers seem to have had a lot of fun with the slow type, but they had more time. Or, at least, they *took* more time.

Be careful, however, to think of pack speed, rather than of the speed of individual hounds. Much night hunting is hound racing which is different from pack hunting, and while we want hounds to "fight for the lead," we don't want them to run jealously nor to be "stingy" with their cry when not out in front.

DRIVE AND GAMENESS

"Drive" is the will to get forward as fast as scent and ground permit. Horsemen refer to a comparable quality as "the will to run." Or as often, they call it "heart." While good conformation and excellent condition are contributory factors, this is an inherent quality, with little outward evidence. But a "top" pack must have it. The quality comes first into evidence in the way a hound harks to cry. If he stands around like a preacher at a barn-raising — momentarily undetermined whether to work or talk, he probably hasn't much drive. But, if when sure of its authenticity he gets to cry at speed, he probably has drive. In a running pack you will see some hounds "run for the front," and the quality which causes them to do this, whether it's the competitive instinct or the urge to give their best to a job, is what we all look for.

"Gameness" is "close kin" to drive. This is the quality which makes men so greatly admire the fighting cock who has it without contamination and untempered by other instincts. The foxhound has it as far as the chase is concerned. He is by no means a game fighter, for a good terrier at a fourth his weight will put him under the barn. But after a fox, when "heart and nerve and sinew" are gone, he will stay in and wring from his exhausted frame the last glimmer of physical energy in the hope that he may outlast the quarry. When you realize that he doesn't eat the fox and doesn't even feel any particular animosity towards that gentleman, this trait shows up in another and truer light. The gamecock fights what appears to him to be a rival for the favor of pullets. He intends to handle the perpetuation of his species in that neighborhood. But the foxhound runs and, if need be, dies for sport alone. There are only three animals that I know of capable of this—a man, a horse, and a hound. A fox maybe, but I can't prove it. He is certainly willing at times to stay above ground and take a lot of punishment when he might as well go in and "call it a day."

We have all had hounds continue in chases after suffering horrible wounds on wire or enduring crippling accidents. But these occasions are the exception rather than the rule, and the foxhunter thinks of a "game hound" as one that won't quit. The hound that gives up for any reason has always had short shrift in this country. A "quitter" blotches the traditions of his parentage, denies himself posterity, brings disgrace to his owner, is shunned like a leper, and frequently terminates his short span at a rope's end, for he commits hunting's one unpardonable sin.

To the hound of quality and sense, the pursuit of the fox is more than sport — it is the raison d'etre. I raised a white bitch once that was a granddaughter of "Big Stride" upon her sire's side and of "Ten Broeck" through her dam. As long as I owned her she had to be kept chained in kennels, for she would climb out of any place and go hunting, and she would run foxes without food or rest until stopped, although the pads of her feet would be worn through to the blood. However, there are many fox hounds that will run their pads off and never stop to eat as long as they can hope to run a fox. Like a gamecock, they have risen above the physical, and neither pain nor wounds can deter them from their single purpose.

HUNTING INSTINCT

Many hounds dislike the task of finding a fox. Some dissemble very cleverly and busy themselves in pastures while their companions work through the briars. Others betake themselves to an inconspicuous spot and stand with head cocked to one side, listening for the signal that says the fun is about to begin. If you can afford it, draft this kind. They frequently run well, but the sight of them is aggravating, and they fail in one important phase of the sport. After all, the fox must be found before he can be run.

Don't expect your young hounds to find foxes, for the best of them do so, chiefly, by accident. And even among the three and four season hounds in the average pack, two or three hounds will find most of the foxes. To begin with, this ability is a compound of long experience, a discriminating nose, and lots of sense. To know where to look, to instantly appraise the value of a line (as to whether the fox was going or coming and how long ago), and to waste no time getting ahead upon the line, depends upon both experience and ability. Also, the good "strike hound" knows the street numbers of all the foxes resident in his community, and if you cast him in that neighborhood, he will have a look-in. But, if you yourself don't know where the foxes live, your casts may often make of finding the fox a problem in the occult.

The day has gone when we were willing to wait while hounds worked out a night line and after hours of tortuous twisting and sonorous baying, got a fox to his feet. Now we don't want hounds to cry a cold line at all. Instead, we demand that he hunt right on over it and try to get at once into the fox's present whereabouts. The beginner at the sport must watch carefully and make sure that his hounds "strike." This is a hunting word of common usage and exactly describes what is wanted, i. e. to strike the line and then go on with it.

CRY

"Such Sweet Thunder"

The foxhound spends a great deal of his time out of the sight of his followers, and a considerable portion of it out of the sight of his fellow hounds. The hunters are dependent upon his cry if they continue to follow the Chase, and the pack is mutually dependent upon cry if it is to play as a team. When hounds are spread out like skirmishers, each with his nose to the ground trying to find the line of a fox, they naturally cannot afford to be watching each other. So, the first hound to catch the scent must tell the others about it. If he doesn't "own it" but slips silently away in order to take the lead, presently the other hounds will be keeping their heads up watching him, or each other, rather than keeping their nose on the ground where they belong. We have no mute hounds to worry about, but we do occasionally have a hound so anxious to run in front that he will steal away and not "open" until he has established a comfortable lead. Hounds quickly learn to ignore the babbler, but the cheat who is trying to steal away on the line cannot be ignored if a pack must work as a team and not as a gathering of jealous competitors.

The character of voice needed is in some degree dependent upon the country. In a wooded and hilly country, the sound waves roll and recoil against the trees and slopes until a little cry seems a big one. But in an open, level country, a greater sound volume is essential. It is a risky thing to breed too "fine mouthed" hounds regardless of their outstanding qualities, for the next generation is likely to have some squeaky voices. To be on the safe side, leave the sopranos alone. The ideal hound voice is one so distinctive in tone that you never mistake it, and one with such volume that it can be heard for great distances, and the real foxhunter stays with hounds by constantly listening to "the music." As the mountain boy who shot the tired fiddler at the dance up near Altamount said to the judge, "Thar hain't nothin' to this dancin' business when the music stops."

Some people follow their friends across country and despair of ever learning how to direct their own course by the cry, or of comprehending what the changes in volume and in tone really mean. But with a little patience, they can identify the tongue of a few reliables and, when hounds are in cover hunting, can visualize the hidden drama of the briars by the orchestration. In the average pack, two or three hounds find ninety per cent of the foxes, so if you know their mouths you are ready for the first act.

A young hound cries, "Fox!" in an excited voice.

"Fox, — fox —" he shouts, makes his way a little further into the wood and shouts again.

"Fox! Fox! . . . I think . . . it's a fox!" His tone now is no longer a bold challenge, it begins even to have a little whine in it.

He is saying now, "Maybe this isn't a fox after all, but just a rabbit that smells like a fox. Now everybody will laugh at me again . . . perhaps I shouldn't cry it at all."

Now comes one of the old dowagers to find what it was that our young friend had cried.

"It is a fox!" she announces, and instantly the woodland noises weave a threnody of excitement. Feet patter in the leaves, young hounds whimper, all scurry to confirm the find. You listen now for another Reliable to confirm the decision, and when that second voice has "honored it," you gather the reins.

The cry grows in intensity and then suddenly seems to lose volume. What's happened? The fox has slipped out into the open. The sound no longer strikes the sounding board furnished by the trees and seems to fade at once. If you want to see the second act, you had better put a rowel between your mule's ribs and be upon your way. But you take a wrong turn in the woodland, come out at a wire fence, blunder back quite a while until you find a gate, and when you do come out into the open, the whole world seems deserted and there isn't a sound to be heard. You suddenly feel that you are alone upon a deserted planet. What shall you do . . . where shall you go? Well, the first thing to remember is that if you stay where you are, the hounds will certainly come back. It's a rare fox that doesn't circle by home in the course of a Chase. Having thus disposed of the "lost feeling," you proceed to cup a hand over your ear and listen. Far to the left, there is sound—but it turns out to be a single housedog railing against monasticism. Then, from down wind and to the right, you distinctly hear the cry of two or three hounds. You canter in that direction for a mile maybe, and upon the top of a hill you rein in and listen. Now you hear hounds! The cry is suddenly much clearer. Why? They have turned your way, and with each leap the sound swells. Which way is the fox going? Listen to the music a moment or two and then lay a course that will meet the arc he is traveling. Now when you slip in behind hounds a couple of miles further on, you are entitled to grin a little, for you have plotted your own course by cry and are no longer shackled to follow the ancients who "know the country." From now on, you begin to enjoy your own interpretations of the music and to recognize the nuances of sound that accompany the swift drama of which we see so little. To really understand cry, to read the story of the Chase from it, you should do a lot of hunting with the "one gallus boys." They are solely dependent upon cry for they see almost nothing of the Chase, but they get its progress with complete accuracy from the sound effects. You sit on a log in silence, surrounded by men you can't see. The night closes around you like a grave. You stir and twist, and marvel at the patience of these listeners. Then, far down in the valley, one hound cries one time and is silent.

"That's Roy Robinson's young bitch. She ain't sure whar that's hit or not," observes a dark shape by your side. More time passes, eons drift by. You are adrift in a black, motionless, soundless void. And then, like a bugle call from the woods just ahead, comes a great challenging cry! There is no indecision about this, no wavering doubts. This is the positive challenge of a warrior announcing that he has found the enemy.

"Be still boys — be still," comes a sibilant whisper from the end of the log. Now the woods are alive. From every direction is heard the patter of feet upon leaves, the grunt and gasp of hounds hurrying to assembly.

A second hound opens.

"Hit's a fox all right," drawls a hitherto silent shape. "Fer that's my ole 'Lucy' and she hain't never told no lie."

The man next to you whispers that the aforesaid "Lucy" will open upon anything from a skunk to a wild hog. Now comes a steady increase of cry as hound after hound "puts in." The line is not "hot enough to run." Hounds must work up on their fox. Suddenly there is no sound.

"The fox crossed through Harold Mitchem's pig lot and that's what's bothering them," your counselor advises.

The cry is resumed by three hounds a goodly distance to the right.

"That's 'Lead,' 'Storm,' and 'Reno.' They hit it ahead in Hardison's cane patch." Presently the three pioneers are joined by nine other hounds, whose voices clearly identify them to the audience.

"Now they have crossed the Natchez Trace at Garrison Schoolhouse and are headed for Sweeny Hollow, — where they cross the branch, that fox will be running," observes the gentle voiced Gus Skelly. And so it goes on through the night. If you graduate from this academy, you can follow hounds in most any country a horse can cross, for the cry ahead will be telling you chapter, book and page of the story. But unless you can interpret cry, unless it is something more to you than just sound, you will always have great difficulty following hounds.

A half century ago all hounds had more or less deep voices, but as the field trial type supplanted the black and tan, or "Red-bone" pioneer type, the great roaring voices became less prevalent, and about fifteen years ago there was a very noticeable weakness in the cry of most well bred hounds. The "fine mouth" and the squeaky one began to be commonplace in most packs, and the 'basso profundo' was rarely heard. In the last few years, hound breeders have been more particular about demanding some volume in the cry of a stallion hound. The improvement has been marked, but I doubt if we will ever regain the great roar of cry that pleased our grandfathers. For one reason, the throaty animal with the dewlaps of a Tammany councilman is not often fast. The speedier hound is more than apt to be clean about the throat, and a deep voice is not, it seems, associated with a finely chiseled throat-latch, nor is it naturally associated with the hard driving fast hound that swings wide at a check. Now and then, one of this type has volume of cry, for example Wooldridge's "Rangoon," but a "coarse chop" is as far down the bass as is to be expected.

A high soprano sometimes has great carrying power, and may be clearly audible over long distances. The fastest hound I ever owned is, or rather was, a bitch called "Stealth," whose voice was very "fine," but she gave it freely at speed and could be heard distinctly when hoarser or deeper voices would no longer carry. However, it is wise to use stallion hounds that have deep voices, for high tones are only tolerable as an abnormality. If a pack has many such voices, the effect is disappointing and individual cry hard to distinguish.

FOX SENSE

Even upon a good scenting day, Br'er Fox may vanish into thin air anytime. Unless good nose is accompanied by "Fox Sense," the hounds upon these occasions might as well be trying to follow a rowboat. "Fox Sense" is not a spiritual affair issued at random from the celestial warehouse by Nimrod, but is just plain "brains." Some families of hounds, like some human families, have a more abundant supply than others. And, naturally, old hounds with several seasons make better use of their experience if they have sense. First season hounds often outrun their elders and look brilliant while the going is good, but at a loss watch them turn towards the veterans of the pack to be rescued.

Many hounds hunt for a lost line all over the place. Watch one with "fox sense" at a loss. He will raise his head and survey the situation just as a man would. And then, he will go galloping off to the first place he thinks the fox might have been likely to go. Perhaps it's a distant clump of woods, the bank of a stream, or a thick fence line along the road. Off he trots, as cool as a cucumber, and not until he gets there does he put his head down. You sit on your horse watching, and a moment later in basso profundo he announces.

"This — is — it — come on boys!"

The smartest man on earth will have a very low batting average on guessing which way a fox went, but a man has to study many things and a foxhound majors in only one subject. It is, however, not only in unraveling scent tangles that a hound shows sense, it is also in finding a fox. Take your young hounds to a strange country and you hardly have a chance to run a fox. But if you also take along an old hound with a lot of sense, you may have a fox up in a short time, for he will hunt in the likely places, and will waste no time at all in pastures and wheatfields, and other such pleasant spots, — that foxes rarely use.

A hound also shows sense in the way he cries a line. Many hounds make almost as much fuss over a cold line as they do over one three minutes old. Watch the smart hound when he picks up a cold line. He doesn't "get in a lather" and bawl his head off. Probably he says nothing at all, but his adrenal glands go to work when that wonderful odor comes to his nose. In an instant he is all attention, and as busy as a Bishop at a christening. Presently, he finds the route the fox traveled when he left. Then, our wise hound speaks, though with deliberation and calm.

"Here-is-a-line — boys," he says, and not much more. You know by his voice exactly what the situation is and about how far he is behind the fox. What a contrast with the rattle-brained hound that announces the Fall of Rome everytime he crosses a night line.

Sense in a hound is displayed in many ways. One of them is in getting out of kennels. The hound that you can't keep in kennels, the one that manages somehow to get over or under the fence, is almost always full of "fox sense." In fact, the hounds that can't be successfully kenneled seem always top hounds. Robert Rodes of Bowling Green once told me that he had a young hound he couldn't keep in kennels, and that he wanted me to see how the hound made his escape. This kennel yard was quite small, not over twenty feet wide, and surrounded by at least a seven-foot wire with three strands of barbed wire strung around the top upon the inside. He put the young hound in the yard along with a number of others and then we walked away to a vantage point for observation. The young hound quietly backed up to the opposite side of the yard, studied the fence a moment, took a stride, made a gigantic leap, seemed to land like a feather among the barbs, was down and free. No one could have made me believe that the leap was possible. I doubted my own eyes. That hound was "Scout" who, six months later, won the First Chase Futurity at Crab Orchard and made himself immortal.

When Joe Thomas decided to make use of the Trigg Blood, I took him to Bowling Green to see Joe Kirby's hounds. We arrived about nine o'clock at night and went to the Kirby Livery Stable. There, in the office, were a little group of contented souls playing "pitch." And, watching the game, was a big, handsome, ringnecked hound. The pack was kept in the mule stalls towards the rear of the stable. We looked them over carefully, and they well deserved it. Inquiry regarding the hound that was "one of the boys" in the card game elicited the response.

"You wouldn't want him. The kennel isn't built that can hold him."

That settled the matter with Thomas. He bought that hound, "Joe Bawley," to head his pack.

Outstanding hounds are generally very individualistic. On the road, they are apt to trot at the head of the pack, or to always take their own position by your horse. "Big Stride," like his master, had the outward manner of greatness. If you saw the Wooldridge Pack coming down the road, you didn't have to ask which hound he was. The hound that gives you a lot of minor annoyance is rarely a real good foxhound. The good ones have too much sense to run cur dogs, bark at stock or to generally "fiddle their time away."

VICES

BABBLING: If your pack is to be kept level in quality, you must constantly be on the watch to weed out those hounds that will harm it. First on the list should be the babbler. The vice of babbling may be tolerated at Washington, but it is ruinous in a good pack. Under the heading of "babblers" come all hounds who "sling their tongues." Generally, this fault is hereditary. Regardless of brilliant performance otherwise, or of beauty, don't breed into families that carry the taint. Babbling apparently is occasioned primarily by vanity. A hound wishes to call attention to himself, to appear important before his mates, so he lies to them about the line. While it is true that the pack learns, long before you do, what hound can be trusted, the babbling hound nevertheless occasions confusion and delay as long as he is in your pack.

Once in a long time an erstwhile reliable old hound begins to "tell a little white lie" now and then. Age has dulled his nose and slackened his speed, and, after a lifetime of honest work, his brothers have confidence in him. So, when he cries that he has found the line, they hasten to him, until in time they find out what he is doing. High strung young hounds in their first season will sometimes develop the vice through nervous anxiety and confusion. For these there is a chance, but, after they have been hunted hard and the novelty of the game has worn off, if they still persist in the vice, they should be drafted.

THE CUTTER OR MR. McCAWBER: This fault is developed through intelligence, perhaps. After numerous trips around and around the hill, old "General" decides to short cut and get closer to Br'er Red. If this strategy proves successful, he begins to cut across lots in earnest and to play hide and seek with the fox. If lucky, he hits the line far ahead of his honest friends toiling behind, and demoralizes them. If he fails, he wanders about upon his own, hoping to distinguish himself by luck rather than by work. So, with a few of the kind, you presently haven't any pack, you just have canny friends willing to go out with you upon the chance of "something turning up."

POOR HUNTERS: If a hound refuses to plunge into the briars and help his comrades look for a fox, but is willing to run after it is up, he has perhaps not committed any great crime. He is like a small boy who waits for the ice cream but won't help his brother turn the freezer. Hunting is work, running is sport, — in the hound world. However, no matter how fast he runs, the hound that is a slack hunter should be drafted. There is no room for a cavalier in a good pack. "No work, no eat," is a well tried motto. There are some hounds that appear to be wonderful hunters; with tails slashing and heads down, they are always on the move, sniffing at everything, — and finding nothing. They mean so well, they want to do their part and help the Club, the Chamber of Commerce, The Sunday School, — the Pack, make new records. But the cunning sinful fellow forever confuses them. They never know where to look for him, — and so they don't find him. The test of a hunting hound is his ability, as the Field Trial Judges say, "to produce his game." Don't be misled by the "busy looking" hound. A fanning tail and a constant sniff at every tuft and humock looks well, but is more apt to indicate a rabbiter than a foxhound. The hound that finds foxes for you is a "good hunter." It's that simple. I like to see a hound busy, and like to see his head down, but — the proof of the pudding is who finds your fox. I had an inbred hound for years by the name of "Mischief." At a cast, he would stand and look up at me with the eyes of a dying calf, apparently in great disapproval of everything I had done. Ahead would be a Kaleidoscopic whirl of hunting hounds. And there would be "Mischief," as immobile as a graven image. Then, I would begin to talk to him in short Saxon words. Finally, he would raise his head, sniff the air a time or two, trot perhaps a half mile across the valley of a branch, disappear in a thicket and come out with a fox! But upon bad scenting days he was, after his fourth year, useless. Then he wouldn't even try to find.

Foxes are not like partridges, and you don't find them by covering the fields with dogs. A good hunting hound looks for his fox where the fox should be. And if he is well trained in pack work, he returns to you and reports failure to find.

"Boss," he says, as plainly as though he used English, "this fox ain't home. Let's go over and try that lemon colored rascal upon the Little Harpeth."

The hound that keeps on trying ahead is a good hunter but a poor pack hound. What you must have is one that hunts where and when you want him to hunt. These Balboa kind of hounds, that headed West to try to discover the Pacific Ocean, are doubtless good hunters, but unless you have a helicopter are perfectly useless. I have known men to take a number of these explorers out, cast them, and never see them again that day. Afterwards, some foxhunter over in Sumner County or somewhere would write a letter and describe the wonderful run that took place. This sort of thing is really rather a common occurrence for men who keep field trial bred hounds. Somehow there has grown up a tradition that the hound that heads North until he either finds a fox or drowns crossing the Ohio River is an ideal hunter. He may be, but most of us prefer one that will answer a horn and report in now and then. No one wants to fatten hogs for strangers to eat.

TOO FAST AND TOO SLOW: The hardest thing in the world to do is to dispose of the hound that is too fast. It should be done, all authorities say, if you are determined to have a really good pack. The hound that runs far ahead is often the best all-around individual, one that comes out of the woods close to his fox, that drives when the scent is good and at a loss, circles wide and fast. This kind is hard to tell goodbye. In fact, they should be "saved for seed." But be sure about the hound that is exceptionally fast. Some "fast" hounds have a trick of stealing away with the line and of not opening upon it at all until they have established a long lead. Others leave the line and appear suddenly ahead of their less astute but more honest comrades.

Many a "fast" hound is a "cutter." Frequently everybody in the county knows this — but the owner.

The hound that gets away far ahead of the pack, and runs there, foils the line for the remainder, and in the end it has hindered rather than helped that

Chase If, however, the hound actually has a better nose, and so can maintain a place far in the lead, it may be that you will want it for breeding purposes. In this event, farm the hound out to someone who is interested in competitive hound running, rather than in a pack's work.

Most honest hounds that run ahead of their fellows seem to do so by wide fast casts at a check. The daring adventurer that circles wide and fast loses little time if he hits it off, and upon each such successful occasion gains a long lead. But many cast themselves too rapidly, overrun the line, and are "thrown out" of the race. An occasional advance runner sets himself forward rather consistently by using his head. At a check, he seems to waste less time nosing about in the wrong places. Perhaps he remembers the run of this particular fox and gets ahead by searching first where the line probably will be. This is the kind to keep and cherish.

But the hound that slips away upon the line, with little cry, is obviously anxious to steal as long a lead as possible, in order to enjoy the distinction of running ahead. A thousand night hunters will trade a good milk cow or a mule for such a hound, and you had better "swap him."

The slow hounds are easy enough to draft, except perhaps an old favorite who has been outstanding in his day, and is now distanced by the competitor that none can defeat — age. Give him to a boy who lives up in the Hills where they both can be happy with grey foxes. But don't punish his stout old heart by keeping him in the pack to be beaten day after day by young hounds.

PERSISTENT RABBITING: This vice, next to babbling, is perhaps the worst. I, myself, am convinced that it is more pronounced in some blood lines than others. Certainly the "Walker hounds with the Wooldridge Class" have slight weakness this way. There is an old controversy on the subject: shall we permit the pups to run rabbits? I can't answer that one, but I have seen many well bred young hounds break themselves of running rabbits before they were a year old. "L'ecstasie" i. e., fox perfume, makes the good ones forget the bunnies. Make sure that your pups are subjected to the early influence of a foxhound, and not walked at a place where rabbit or varmint dogs are kept. This is the only certain way to start them out right. An old foxhound will soon teach pups the true faith.

If you can't soon break a hound of rabbiting, get rid of him before he corrupts the good manners of others. Nothing is as demoralizing as not knowing, when a hound opens, whether he is crying fox. Old hounds with this

"GONE AWAY!"

Give him to a boy who lives up in the hills.

vice are worthless, I fear. The night hunter's hounds sometimes run a fox "true" at night, and rabbit in the daytime. But a good red fox hound despises the short circles of a grey fox, — to say nothing of a rabbit. Don't breed to hounds with this vice; don't even raise puppies around dogs that rabbit. Use the thong when your young hounds trail a rabbit, and you will be reasonably free from this annoyance, except during a short period in the early Spring, when hounds at times seem unable to resist the allurement. Some hunters say that during the Spring rut of the rabbit the hound is often confused by the scent. I doubt that, but have long noticed that the best hounds may be unsteady for a week or two at this period of the year.

CRYING A COVERED LINE: When a pack has a good scent and is driving a fox, the hounds that are behind should not lower their noses and attempt to work the line themselves. If they do this the fault is generally referred to as "crying a covered track." There is no difference of opinion among hunters as to this fault, except as to how far behind a hound is entitled to be before he should stop giving tongue and devote himself solely to the task of getting forward. Upon a good scenting day if a hound is beyond ten rods to the rear many of us believe he should be concerned about getting forward, and should keep his mouth shut until he gets closer. Upon a day when the line is hard to handle and frequent losses occur, we doubtless should not be overly critical of the hound that cries twenty-five rods to the rear for he has perhaps been obliged to stoop to the line several times and is loath to delegate the duty to his comrades ahead.

But the hound that regularly refuses to honor his brothers' testimony, and comes bawling along behind the pack, should be drafted.

FAILURE TO HARK TO CRY: The hound that doesn't hark readily to cry is either getting old, or is an honest gentleman living among cheats, or is an egocentric disinterested in any other evidence than that he himself obtains. An old campaigner among a group of recruits is apt to ignore their challenges, — and be right about it. But the fox-hound that doesn't hark quickly to the cry of the seasoned and reliable members of the pack greatly hampers its work. He is on a *team* and must work with it; so when a teammate identifies a line he must gallop quickly to his support, get his nose down and attempt to get in the play. In a pack of Walker hounds this means the use of a lot of energy, for they will scatter over a wide area when searching for a fox.

There are few more beautiful sights in hunting than the scene that develops when a trusted leader first cries, "fox," — up go the heads of his fellows, here, there, and everywhere throughout the cover. When he confirms discovery, hounds start at a gallop for him, and their white markings gleam against the green cedars and red buck-brush as they hasten to cry.

Hounds that hunt in wooded hills become slack about getting to cry, particularly if foxes are plentiful. It is too easy for a hound to start his own fox, or to join the chase the next time it comes by. There is no question but that hounds determined to run their own quarry should be whipped off and put in after the fox the pack is running, nor should a hound be allowed to lag in getting to cry, — when the fox is up. However, until a definite line has been established it is well to be slow about harking hounds, — unless discovery is announced by a veteran who has your complete confidence.

With well bred hounds not past their prime, the cure for slackness in getting on to cry is to hunt them in open and reasonably level country, where Brother Fox is apt to set his neck straight and go away. The hound that waits for him to circle back finds himself all alone in a silent world, and, being by nature gregarious, immediately feels lost and neglected, quits his individual explorations and harks to the first cry he hears. A few more days of this and he becomes a much better pack hound.

SHAPE

A hound that is beautiful is so shaped that he moves easily. To do this, he must be symmetrical. That is, his neck, legs, back, etc., must not only be individually right but they must be all made for the same model. Then the parts will fit together so that there will be less wear and tear.

The head is a very important point. This is true in all animals, including man. The head and eye furnish the only outward indication of character and temperament. Years ago, I knew a Kaw Indian by the name of Pappan who was a marvelous judge of horseflesh. When I asked him for the secret of his power of discernment, he replied:

"My father told me that when I went to look at a horse to put a blanket over all of him but his head. If his head was good, take the blanket off and look at him; if the head was bad, no need to take off the blanket." A large headed hound might have a lot of sense, but running a fox is not a problem in algebra. It is a game, not a business. For that matter, probably neither a foxhound nor a foxhunter should be too quickminded. If the former has brains, he learns to cut across the woods pasture and meet the fox, instead of playing "follow the leader" up and down the creek. And if the foxhunter has brains, he is an anomaly. And eventually, he stops hunting because he gets lonesome.

The neck is of great importance in any animal called upon to move at great speed. Did you ever see a shortnecked thoroughbred horse, wild goose, gamecock, deer or antelope? The neck should be long, a little swan-shaped, and without throatiness. A slight curve at the crest, such as you see upon highly bred horses, adds greatly to the hound's appearance. Nor should the neck be large at its base, for neither a thoroughbred horse nor a hound is designed to pull a load. But of still greater importance is the fact that long necks are rarely seen with bad shoulders. And well-sloped, cleancut shoulders are essential for quick and easy movement. A straight shoulder means slow movement.

The back and loins should be strong and the pelvis should be wide. An arched, or wheel back, is not to be confused with "goose rump." The latter is a sign of weakness rather than of strength. Strong loin muscles are of vital importance; speed and stamina are both dependent upon the development of these muscles. Most of our hounds are not well developed in the loins. They seem to compensate for the deficiency in loin muscle by good arched backs. The combination of these two provides an ideal system for the transmission of power.

A wide pelvis means that the hound stands with his hindquarters apart, and this is an indication of plenty of strength. The hound with a narrow pelvis stands and runs with his hindquarters close together, and this means weakness. Bench show judges agree that hounds should not be very long in the back, but the "National" rules say "moderately long," which is probably right. A short-coupled hound like a short-backed horse "looks better," but top speed seems to more frequently occur with moderate length.

The ribs should be flat but well sprung, and with plenty of depth to the barrel. Without such depth, a hound appears "leggy" and certainly lacks stamina.

The underline should curve up somewhat, but not like a greyhound's. A "tucked up" underline suggests speed but not staying power, and hounds with great stamina are rarely so built. But the straight underline marks the "tub of guts" kind and is even less desirable.

That a hound should stand straight on his forelegs is now almost everybody's opinion, but until Doomsday this will undoubtedly be one disputed point, for that straightness is a point of utility is debatable enough; and the issue doubtless will continue to occasion "killings" in Tennessee and Kentucky during the coming century. The elbows must be parallel to the plane of the body, neither turned out nor in. The pasterns should slope slightly, for that slope is contributory to speed. In past years, many of our hounds have had too much slope in the pastern, so far as bench show rulings have been concerned. And it takes a rather straight pastern to get a judge's nod. But to run a *fox* is another matter. A straight hind leg is likewise agreed upon. It is certainly better looking, although its essential utility may be debatable. All hunters agree that the hocks should be low; that the length should be from hip to hock, with little from the hock to the ground. But to win the approval of hunters or judges, a hound must by all means "stand up on his hocks."

The rules give plenty of latitude about the foot. Hunters like a round, compact, catlike foot. The general feeling is that this type of foot wears better and is less troubled by broken or fallen arches. The foot that is "spread out" early in the hound's career has little chance of withstanding the hard punishment of high speed and hard ground for a term of years. When nature developed the horse, she did not give him an adequate circulatory system in his legs, and most of his training is a struggle to keep leg sound. The foxhound has no basic weakness of the sort, and few animals excel him in physical balance. But of course he too is a racing machine, and his feet come in for a devil's tattoo. There is no foot pattern that suits all teritories. Judge Bob Thompson at Gulfport, Mississippi, whose good hounds are in the swamps half the time needs, I daresay, size and spread in his hounds' feet. But Chief Dave Ware, hunting the sandstone hills of the Osage Nation, must need a tough and compact foot on his hounds if they are to keep going.

The stern is of more importance than is generally conceded. It is not only the banner under which the craft sails, but to some degree the rudder. The tail should be thick at the root with a considerable flag, be curved like a saber and be carried high. It should be habitually carried high, — in fact, never be lowered. The present day custom at bench shows of holding up a hound's tail while the judge looks at him robs the game and proud hound of all his natural advantage. The great hound carries his stern up. Only this kind should be bred to. Nothing improves the appearance of a hound, or of a pack, more than "flying a high flag." If a foxhound won't naturally walk with pride, he should be given to a negro boy to run varmints. The fox himself never lowers his brush, unless he is dead beat.

The size of a foxhound is controlled to a very considerable degree by what his dam had to eat, and how he was fed during his first six months. Provided a hound has balance, symmetry, and a rugged frame, size is not a matter of great importance. Br'er Fox is not a big fellow. However, if your country has any amount of woven wire fencing, the smaller you breed your hounds, the better. Likewise, in a thickly grown up country, the small hound has an advantage. Such country is generally used by grey foxes, and small hounds follow their corkscrew course with greater ease.

When conformation is discussed, foxhunters frequently defend their fondness for a beautiful hound by insisting that it takes a proper shaped one to run well. Perhaps it does. Certainly, it takes a long necked one to get his head to the ground with ease. But that it takes straight legs, I have my doubts. Certainly the fox isn't straight! Nor has he any abundance of bone!

Foxhunting is a sport; an old, colorful and picturesque one in which beauty is entitled to have a major part. Regardless of what you or I think about the values of virtue and the worth of wisdom, beauty continues to be the most sought after of all qualities. A big-eyed girl, sculpt to the popular taste, will generally draw a larger salary in pictures than we pay our President. And more people go annually to see the Great Smoky National Park than have visited Pennsylvania steel mills since the war between the States. So you should exercise your own predilections as to the shape, color, and size of your hounds. But if you want them to run together, their size and shape should be of a pattern.

The standards set out by the National Foxhunters' Association are undoubtedly the best we have. They represented the composite opinion of a carefully chosen group of able men, well qualified by both experience and intelligence, to say what the shape of a hound should be. If, however, you disagree with these standards, you should modify them to suit your own taste. We don't make much progress just following the other fellow in circles. A foxhunting soldier boy, just home from North Africa, told me recently that when the Arab caravans left for the desert, it was always at sundown, and as soon as they were started on the trail, the drivers went to sleep and the camels followed in the footsteps of the lead camel. So our boys hit upon the brilliant idea of sneaking up and starting the lead camel in a circle, and then when the sun came up, the awakening Arabs, irate and astonished, found themselves just where they started.

I know exactly how a Sheik feels under such circumstances, for like many other hound breeders, I have often confused motion with progress. In truth, the task of modifying hound shape without sacrifice of hunting qualities is more than a summer's dalliance, — it is nearer a lifetime of effort with no assurance at all of success.

The important thing about a pack is that it works as a unit.

CHAPTER V

THE PACK

The ideal pack of hounds would be almost equal in speed and in drive. This would make it advisable to have them all as nearly the same size and shape as possible. Such a pack should swing with their fox as a unit, and at a check, should fan out into a line of skirmishers. Then when a hound regained the line, the rest of the pack would close upon him at speed and be off again. The more evenly hounds were matched the better the pack would be, and to accomplish this, hounds would have to be bred very much alike. To keep them level in speed, it would be necessary to draft the slow ones from time to time and to hunt the extremely fast ones separately. I have done the former time without end, but the latter is always a difficult thing to do.

The size of a pack, like the size of a fireplace, is apparently somewhat a matter of taste. But both are determined to a considerable degree by the country of your residence. In an open country without large woodlands, ten couples of really good hounds doubtless would, as the darkies say, make any fox "ball the jack." In a country of big woods, a larger pack might be better, provided it is made up of good hounds. Oddly enough, in a hill country that isn't too wooded, a very small pack does well, for hill foxes circle a great deal. Then, too, cry is much better in hilly country. These conditions make it possible for hounds that get thrown out to get back in with no great difficulty. If your children insist upon higher education, and your wife is determined to go to town to shop every few months, you can personally economize in a hill country, by keeping only five or six couple of top hounds, and still may have good sport.

The greatest mistake made by Masters of organized packs is that they keep numbers rather than quality. A dairyman or a poultry raiser constantly culls the non-producers. A man must be indifferent both about money and hounds to keep the ones that lend their moral support. Probably twenty couple of *good* hounds is as many as were ever under one aegis since Time began. However, the Treasury Department seems to have become interested in the size of packs, and apparently the large pack is soon to join the large diamond in the dim vaults of Victorian memory. But the man who keeps few hounds is much more apt to keep good ones, so we may yet be grateful for the Income Tax.

When a pack of hounds is running a fox, it should run bunched, like running horses turning into the stretch, rather than in a column like cows in a lane. At a loss, it should open like a fan, so that the line may be more quickly picked up. This way of running is aptly called "carrying a good head," and the phrase describes it. When you see a pack run in this fashion, you may know that it is balanced as to speed and ability.

When a pack is composed of slow, as well as of fast hounds, it functions in just the opposite manner. Running, it tails out into column, and at a check, the weaker, and the doubting brethren, concern themselves with verifying the reports of the leaders, by loud "amens." Years ago it was not an unusual thing to see a pack of hounds, tied to a scent, boo-hooing across the country in a long line, each one making sure for himself that the scripture and text were correct. With the development of the Field Trials came the modern short-eared hound that cast wide at a check, and took chances with the line. As an individual, he is infinitely superior, but as a pack hound, some have glaring faults, and to some degree, run *at* the line, rather than with it. By taking a chance at the losses, striking the line ahead now and again, this type hound, upon his good days, pushes a fox in a dramatic and beautiful fashion. But when scent is spotty, and "ole Red" twists and turns and changes his mind, the picture is sometimes less attractive.

A pack should run *with* the line, not *at* it. Hounds should turn with the line, and not frequently go beyond it. (To run a fox is one thing, *to race hounds* is another). You often hear the expression "they are carrying the line." That is just what you want a pack to do.

Once, years ago, I was hunting with the King of Foxhunters, and we sat upon our horses at the edge of a wood facing a field of shocked corn. From a little distance came the mounting roar of the pack in full cry. There was a patter in the leaves, a tawny flash, and out of the wood and straight down the corn rows ran the fox. In the middle of the cornfield, he made a quick and perfect right angle turn and continued his flight. Into the wood swept the pack and rocked the world with their cry. As they came out into the cornfield, "Flying Cloud" was in the lead, the scent was breast high and he was running as fast as he could put his feet down. When he came to the spot where the fox had changed directions, "Flying Cloud" turned so quickly himself that he rolled over and over before he could get going in the new direction. This was absolute perfection in running *with* the line. His descendants, to a surprising degree, inherited his aptness at following a fox. When a *pack* runs with the line in such a fashion, a fox must either catch a ride upon the "Pan American," run like the devil for the home-plate, or be tagged.

In many packs, there are three or four brilliant, wide-casting hounds that run in front and don't mind running over the line. Behind them the pack hounds, somewhat confused by the speed and cry of the gentry ahead, make a slower and more careful attempt to run *with* the line. When the front hounds overrun, as they frequently do, the pack hounds often, upon bad scenting days particularly, puzzle out the line and enjoy the transitory glory of announcing discovery. But more frequently, when scent is good, a wide casting hound intercepts the line ahead and is "out in front" by a long lead, while his discomfited brethren are still trying to come through on the route that the fox traveled. Now neither of these approaches is a correct one. The fast, wide casting hound is the very one who runs over when the fox makes sharp turns or runs his foil. Conversely, the hound that tries to puzzle out the actual route of the fox delays the chase beyond all hope of a quick burst, if the fox is a straight runner.

48   "GONE AWAY!"

Flying Cloud turned so quickly that he rolled over and over.

The ideal pack would include neither one nor the other kind of hound, but would be made up of hounds of uniformly good speed, which at a check would neither scatter to the four winds nor emulate the bloodhound's patient ways. The important thing about a pack is that it works as a unit. Its usefulness is impaired if its members are jealous and independent. A collection of wonderful musicians is not perforce an orchestra. Nor are a group of excellent hounds a pack. And to run a fox hard, you must have team play among your hounds. When one recovers a fragment of the line and in quavering tones says, "Owh - o, here - is - part of it," his comrades in arms must not continue jealously upon their own inquiries, but must think, "Good old 'Lead,' he has something. I'll go help him."

Nor can they ever drive the Red Wraith if strung out in a long column. It is true that our nine year old "Trusty," a mile back, may in time catch up at a bad loss and unravel the tangle. But meantime, the fox has put a lot of ground between himself and the hounds. To drive a fox, a pack must swing upon his line, and when a loss is picked up, it must not be scattered like hens shadowed by a hawk. Many a good hound, making his own wide cast, gets well settled on the line before he says anything. And he has but one purpose in view, i. e. to steal a long lead upon his comrades. Now, he is probably a wonderful individual, but he isn't designed for pack work, any more than is the slow, snuffling, white waist-coated old codger who tries to verify the exact route of the fox and to make canine depositions before a Notary every time his "Red Majesty" changes direction.

"How," asks the neophyte, "do I train a pack to perform the right way?" The answer is the same one by which the orchestra leader and the football coach coalesce individuals into units of their groups, — by practice. Exercise your hounds together every day, take them for walks, hunt them in open country. Hunting hounds in wooded mountainous country develops individuality and not pack habits. Night hunting in the summertime is a wonderful way to break the young entry to fox and to keep the older ones fit, but it is certainly not helpful to pack work. Too much opportunity exists for hounds to branch off singly or in small groups. However, if carried on in moderation, the benefits outweigh the disadvantages unless your pack is made up of the field trial type. In that case, it might perhaps be better to avoid night hunting until you have your pack well in hand and running as a unit.

No amount of training will develop a pack of hounds, however, unless it be composed of individuals that are much alike in size, speed and temperament. This practically means that they must be bred from kindred strains.

"It sounds like a big order," as the farmer's son replied to his father upon being told to come home the last day of the County Fair by milking time. And it is a big order. That is why there are so few good packs.

One of the best packs I ever saw drive a fox was made up of three litters from the same sire and dam. They not only looked alike but ran alike, and the fox that stayed out in front of those hard driving campaigners knew that "he had been someplace" when the chase was over.

Biscuits are the trainers' trick.

CHAPTER VI

TRAINING

DISCIPLINE

A favorite uncle of mine used to say that the best place to raise a boy is on the deck of a battleship. And he further concluded that without stiff discipline, you couldn't raise an able one. Hounds are much like boys, they require control in their youth if you want them to amount to something in age. The South is full of good hounds. In my humble opinion, most of the world's really great individual hounds are produced in Kentucky, Tennessee, and the borders of adjoining states. But these hounds are frequently headstrong and uncontrolled. And they are difficult to discipline because of an excess of timidity. You know plenty of kennels where hounds watch the yard gate just exactly as so many penned-up wolves would. If it's left momentarily ajar, they dash out and are gone. Many of them require a search party to follow up every hunt. A large proportion are not horn-broken. They will come to a horn when *they* get ready, not sooner. As for their master's voice, — it might as well be Balaam's Ass braying, for all they notice. Few of these dashing gentry approve the names they have received and are absolutely indifferent to any summons. You might call them until sun up but would awaken no more response than the echoes. Then, there are hounds that can't be taken out of the kennel except on a leash. To take these hounds for a walk would be as impossible as taking a similar number of wildcats for a stroll. You may have seen men who had to put a leash upon a hound before they could take him out of kennels. I have a picture of a great foxhunter and breeder of top hounds showing his pack, — all upon leash. The leathers come back to his hands as though he were driving the "20 mule team" of the old Borax Company. In the field, these same hounds will push on a line like the "Robert E. Lee" would the Mississippi current, but they hunt where *they* want to hunt and their master follows. They are rarely ready to come home with him but, like roistering negroes on Saturday night, stay out until daybreak ends the fun. Of course, when hounds stay out because they can never get enough hunting, it is a great testimonial to their breeding, if not to their training.

If you are starting with a small pack of undisciplined hounds, you first teach them their names. Perhaps the best way to do this is to toss them biscuits or cracklings and to call out their names as you do. Next after feeding, take your young hound for a walk. It is here that an old and disciplined hound is of great help. As the daily walks progress, add to the number of hounds that go out, until presently you are able by the help of pockets full of biscuits and some cajolery to walk the pack out for a little while.

I hope that upon these occasions you are of a calm turn of mind, for now and then a startled bunny will wave his white flag and most of the pack will throw schooling to the winds. Or a hound here and there will, for no reason, slip under a gate or through a stile and be gone. Don't let these desertions greatly annoy you. After all, this is not Germany, and even a hound has some right to individuality. But don't walk hounds out at dawn, when the mists are in the valleys and "scornful day represses — night's vain and void caresses," for then a hound can rarely resist the lovely scents that call him away from the drill ground.

Now you start teaching hounds to follow your horse. First, you go out with three or four hounds and gradually increase the number. If you have difficulty, take them night hunting, feed them well upon their return, and *then* take them out for training. Hounds quickly learn, especially by example, and a pack that will obey your bidding on the road is not too difficult to train. However, if your hound exercise takes place, of necessity, in a fenced up country when hounds may leave you helpless to reach them, the task is a far more difficult one, for rabbiting and truantism are then harder to punish. If possible, exercise your hounds in areas where you can get to them upon these occasions and can enforce your voice with the bite of the thong. A hound is no violet. He is a savage cousin of the wolf and, with proper support from his fellows, will kill anything that crosses his path. I don't believe in cruelty, nor subscribe to the lap dog treatment. Make your hounds respect your authority. When they ignore your commands and horn, see that they get a touch or two on the backside. You have to be fair with hounds, but you also have to be firm, — if you expect any obedience.

To take undisciplined hounds out in a country filled with lambs, calves, chickens and cur dogs is, as one of my delicate neighbors says, like taking a "male cow" in a china shop. When you are confronted with such crimes as running sheep or other livestock, only prompt and rigorous punishment will serve. Catch the principal culprit in *flagrante delicto* and flog him until your arm aches. The cur dog problem is less difficult, but more frequently confronts a huntsman. There should be a law against anybody keeping a "cur dog," i. e. any other breed than a foxhound, but since there is as yet no legal protection in the matter, hounds must be trained to ignore them. Frequently hounds form the habit of running a certain dog, generally one owned by a choleric landowner always on the verge of putting up "no trespass' signs. They are on the qui vive as they approach the spot where "Fido" waits, and are away after him in an instant. To cure this, station someone ahead with a pistol and as the hounds charge around the house, fire the gun in their faces. Nothing upsets a foxhound like noise, particularly the report of a gun, and if his sport is interrupted a few times by one, he will find less pleasure thereafter in attempting to massacre a lone dog. What a foxhound likes is ten to one odds in his favor. At lesser odds, he can be a great coward. We had a wire-haired terrier years ago that not only faced a pack of forty hounds with audacity, but even finally intimidated most of them.

Rabbit running is, of course, more strictly a problem in the field. When hounds are out for exercise and up pops a "cottontail," they, of course, suffer great temptation, — as would you and I upon many occasions if a porterhouse steak appeared from the daisies and hopped across the meadow. But it is upon such occasions that you really have an opportunity by generous use of the lash to break young hounds. Always use the same expression upon these occasions. "Leave it" is an easily said and useful one, though many able hound men always add "rabbit" to it. It seems silly to be so particular about the words you use, but it is a matter of importance, for a hound is no linguist. My True-love tells me that her French Poodle understands one hundred words, but I fear that a foxhound, like a football player, is better facing goal posts than blackboards, and the fewer words he must know, the better.

All hounds should answer to their names and to their master's horn. The hound that refuses to come to the horn is the greatest nuisance in the world and causes endless annoyance. We are all familiar with the problem: Fifteen miles from home, getting dark, starting to sleet, all hounds in but "Van Dyke," and he is across an impassable ravine amusing himself with a cold line. You blow until your lips are numb and finally depart knowing that the next day you, or somebody, will have to come back and inquire at a dozen farms and probably get no word of this free agent. Then in about a week, you get a postcard from over on South Harpeth containing the news that "Van Dyke" is tied in Ezra Lightfoot's barn and will you please come and get him — "he has already eaten four of my wife's finest hens, the four we showed at the County Fair last summer."

Breaking hounds to the horn is obviously a difficult thing in countries marred by wire, forests, and mountains. If no one can get to the hound, he, of course, does as he pleases. But if he knows that a whip may enforce the summons, he presently learns to come when he hears the horn. And if, when he comes in, you toss him a biscuit, you have established the basic principle of all discipline, i. e. punishment for disobedience and reward for complying with the rules.

The established pack that has only this year's entry to train has a great advantage, for the example of the old is swift training for the young. But to start with an absolutely green pack, in which no hound has manners nor training, is a heart breaking job. I have done it several times in my life and looking backwards, am aghast at my own audacity. Upon two of these occasions, I had neither hounds of any experience, nor men who had even seen a kennel. The situation was like that of my old C. O., Colonel H......, an irascible graduate of the Indian Campaigns, who was once sent to the Philippines to train a regiment of constabulary cavalry. The assignment was not particularly to the Colonel's liking. In fact, he, I fear, had the Irish trait of perpetual indignation. After some weeks, he skipped over military channels and sent to Washington this memorable wire: "Have a thousand horses that have never seen a man, and a thousand men who have never seen a horse, — and twelve officers who have never seen either. What shall I do?"

I would suggest to the young man who faces such a problem that he ask the M. F. H. of some pack that has hounds under control to loan him five couple of old hounds for the summer months. Any Master would be glad to do this. With five couple of thoroughly broken hounds as a training squad, double that number of young hounds may be schooled if divided into small groups each day and put with the old hounds at road work, for walking out, etc.

The young hound who is taken out with old hounds only is schooled to reasonable manners and like a boy with a group of middle aged men, he tries hard to conduct himself with dignity. But if there are two boys, some light skirmishing will develop. And, for each additional boy added, the influence of the older men's behavior will lessen. When a young hound goes out for roadwork, don't let your assistants gallop after him and crack whips when he makes a dash to leave the pack. If no rebel joins him, he will presently come meekly back. It is only when two or three hounds make a break for liberty that correction is demanded.

Kennel discipline has the same basic principle, but should depend more on reward than punishment. Nine out of ten hounds are very anxious to do just what they think we want of them, but we don't always understand what goes on in the hound's mind. An old story illustrates the point. It was a cold night, and two hounds scratched outside their master's door, begging for admittance. Time dragged by and indoors the master, with his feet to a roaring fire, read his paper in comfort.

"Why doesn't he let us in," whined the young hound.

"He will," answered the old one. "He's just slow-minded, that's all. I have been trying for years to make him understand that when I scratch at the door, it means I want him to open it."

You should take your pack for a walk every day you don't hunt. If you have never done this, start out with one steady hound and a pocket full of biscuits. Then day by day add to the number you walk out. If some young hound gives you trouble, take him out by himself, particularly when he is hungry, and snap a biscuit at him every now and then. He will soon learn that a walk is not a hunt and will enjoy it as much as you do. Now and then you get a hound born a rogue, one that is determined to do as he pleases. Get rid of him, because breaking him will ruin your nerves. Like a "horsemule colt" he is the devil's grandson, and will always seek ways of sin. Life is too short to spend a year or two of it trying to break one hound of vice.

The question of the use of the whip is a difficult one. Many packs would be better off if the whips were hung over the picture of the late Master, and left there to gather dust. Whips are like spurs, not one man in ten knows how to use them, — but for that one man they are of great value. A hound's nerves are generally more upset by the bark of a whip than by its bite. Be easy about cracking it. The "pop" of a whip should be the herald of punishment. Running sheep is the number one vice and demands the lash. If an old hound is guilty of this you can send him to the Gulf Coast, or destroy him. If the offender is a young one, a severe flogging is the kindest thing you can do. Beat him until your arm fails, for only a bowl of this tea will save him from future lead poisoning. During one season, the Hillsboro Hounds had an outbreak of sheep running that threatened to destroy the pack. It was solved by our hard riding Secretary, John Sloan, who then was also riding as First Whip. He armed himself and the Second Whip with shotgun pistols, and every time a hound turned after sheep, he received a few birdshot in the posterior, — to remind him of life's obligation. Few hounds ever had the second treatment of this allopathic remedy, and within a short time the pack renounced evil, and was "living a Christian life."

A foxhound is like a child, many times when you think he is disobeying you he is only preoccupied with other interests, and your voice isn't registering upon his consciousness. Suddenly, he is bludgeoned by a shouting man upon a giant horse and, of course, runs away in dire confusion, totally innocent of what it is all about.

The real basis of training a pack is first, as my friend, Eugene Harris says, "to hunt the devil out of them." Whipping the devil out is a much more awkward process. The summer before your young hounds are entered into the pack, they should be run three times a week, if possible. Of course, this has to be at night. Then they come into the pack conscious that this is a serious business, and instead of running every rabbit and cow they see, they will look for fox.

I like to feed young hounds before I walk them out. If their bellies are full, they are less likely to be interested in sudden dashes and forays, and are inclined to go along with the pack in an orderly manner.

When you take hounds out for exercise, don't let your assistant, whoever he is, go galloping, shouting and whip cracking after a hound when he darts away from the pack. A hound is full of insatiable nasal curiosity. He must go smell things. Leave him alone and nine times out of ten when he sees the pack disappearing he will come bounding back into its midst. For a foxhound, like a horse, is very gregarious, particularly when young, and doesn't ordinarily like to find himself alone. The most general and widespread mistake of men, experienced or otherwise, who attempt to discipline a pack, is to get excited when a hound leaves it. It is a simple thing to make a pack of hounds follow a horse in close formation. All this takes is daily road work and correction in liberal doses, and presently the pack will crowd each other like sheep going into a barn. But to train a pack to trot along *in front* of your horse, heads and sterns up, with both gaiety and responsiveness in their bearing, is more difficult. Bits of dog biscuit are to hound training what chunks of meat are to lion training, — indispensible. Fill your pocket with biscuits when you go into the kennel, and when you leave, leave it with the hounds. Call a hound by name now and then and at the same time, toss him a biscuit. It is a magic touch and its charm works most of the time. For the few hounds who are indifferent to this lure, I recommend pork cracklings, — no hound's spiritual urges rise above his appetite for these morsels.

Many hounds are shy about being handled. They may only be cured of this timidity by handling. Tie such a one by the kennel door and stroke his head every time you pass. Take him out alone for a walk when you have time, and soon he will trust you as confidently as would a shepherd dog.

Training hounds hunting ahead of you in the field to change direction when you do is, of course, vital in handling a pack. Hounds learn to do this after your voice has laid them upon the line a few times. They then begin to recognize you as a help in the game, and to associate discovery of the fox or recovery of the line with you. When you have proven that your assistance is occasionally of value, the young hound listens for your voice and relates his direction to yours. When this has been accomplished, he is well upon his way to being a pack hound.

The training of foxhounds, like the schooling of birddogs, is an arduous task, and unless you have an unflagging interest in it, is a difficult thing to accomplish. But its rewards are great. To take the field with a brilliant pack that responds to your signals and pushes Br'er Fox "all out" is one of the most exhilarating things that a man ever learns to do.

SCHOOLING

One time some years ago when "The National" met at Charlottesville, Virginia, a dispute arose in interpreting the procedure at the Cast. The disputants finally agreed to arbitrate, and a distinguished Virginian was invited to decide the matter. He listened patiently to the technical verbage offered and then, in these succinct words, gave his decision:

"Gentlemen, my interpretation of the rules is that we put hounds down and let 'em run." His suggestion pretty well describes the training procedure normally followed with the average small pack. However, the care that is exercised with the training of a young hound is directly reflected in the quality of the sport he later provides.

When the pups are about eight months old, select a remote farm, occupied by an old fox hunter, and put with him from four to six pups and one or two absolutely honest old foxhounds, that you know won't run anything but a fox. Don't expect your old friend to provide the feed, for if he has been long a hunter, he hasn't the money. And, unless he is white, and you are sure about him, don't provide the money for feed. I have done that many times, only to later discover that the money bought, "escape for a prisoned soul," but not cornbread for pups. You must provide the actual hound feed. This might as well be calculated so that there is also enough cornmeal and cracklings to feed the family. Or better, use prepared dog food meal, to be mixed if possible with milk, and supplemented with pork cracklings.

If the country is a "grey fox" one, so much the better. Those twisting, dodging, circling rascals provide ideal schooling for young hounds. And seldom do they run far enough to break a pup's heart. Moreover, if a youngster gets thrown out of a run, he has a dozen chances to get back in. In such an environment, unkennelled, the young hounds will run fox for day after day, and, within a short time, be totally indifferent to all else. After four to six months of this, when about fourteen months old, you may bring them back to the pack. They now know how to hunt and to run a fox, but may or may not know about following a horse, and coming to the horn. So this training must be started at once.

As with undisciplined older hounds, the first thing to do is to fill your pockets with broken biscuits or cracklings, and walk the youngsters out from the kennel. Toss bits to them before you open the kennel door. Then, open it and stand there, continuing to feed them. Walk away a few yards, and back into the kennel again, continuing meantime to call them by name and to toss feed their way. Gradually, day by day, extend your walks. Don't be flustered when two or three barge off as though determined to leave the country. Instead, call them, tap your horn a couple of short notes and at once start off in the opposite direction. Meantime, keep talking to those near you and feeding them. "Patience does it." Presently, your pack of pups will go walking with you anywhere, playing along in front of you, changing direction when you do, and with half an ear cocked for the sound of your voice and horn. Now, have a man on a horse go with you a few times, until they are thoroughly accustomed to the animal. After that, you may exercise them with the pack, either afoot or horseback.

On the days when you don't hunt, your hounds should have an hour's exercise, preferably on the lanes, or otherwise in large open fields. Out of hunting season three or four hours is necessary to maintain discipline and condition. Biscuits are the trainer's trick. Hounds expecting an occasional reward are forever keeping an ear cocked for your voice. When you change direction, touch your horn. Vary both the route and the pace. Now and then break into a brisk trot and occasionally into a sharp gallop. Hounds love this.

The next step is to teach hounds to stop at the command, "back." Only this word should be used, none other. When you use it, turn your horse in the opposite direction. Repeat the lesson over and over, week after week, until it is understood.

The other necessary command is "move over!" In these days, you are sure to meet an automobile upon even the most remote lane, and only the pack trained to move quickly to the side of the road upon command is safe. Every time you meet a car, signal it to slow down, and ride to the side of the road as far as possible, repeating at the same time the one order, "move over!" Even a flock of sheep can be taught this, so there is no reason to despair of teaching it to hounds. The learning may be expedited if you have a man carrying a long whip approach in a car, with instruction to make the laggards jump as he goes by. The kindest thing you can do for a hound is to teach him to fear an automobile and to dislike a road.

To make hounds handy and responsive to your direction, let them go along the lane ahead of your horse, and when you come to a crossroad, turn down it, — touching your horn once, or signaling with your voice, as you do so. Soon you will see your hounds watching you at the crossroads, and presently in the field they will change direction out ahead of you whenever you turn your horse another way.

Training hounds to heed the horn is difficult in a mountainous or big wooded country, chiefly because it is frequently so difficult to hear. The long moaning notes of the homing call, repeated over and over, and supplemented by the voice with long drawn out "Come Away — Come Away — home," succeed better than other calls. But still, we have myriads of good hounds that pay it little attention. However, when the fox has gone to ground, or has been lost, "and the late is about to catch us," a hound will almost always stop to listen. If he knows that in your pocket is a biscuit which he will receive upon arrival, the horn has an added significance. Nothing is more vital than that your hounds come to your horn. Without this accomplished, fox hunting terminates always in annoyance. And the risk of good hounds coming home alone on a road is, in most countries, a frightful one. If you can "squeal your horn," use the wildest squeal in it for the moments when the fox is up and the crash of cry commences. If you can't squeal it, "double" on it with a staccato burst of wild sharp notes that you never used upon any other occasion. This is, of course, to assemble the pack and to get them forward on the line. The basic purpose of the horn is to draw hounds to you, and, contrarywise, the huntsman uses his voice in most cases to encourage hounds forward and away from him.

Your pack of foxhounds should not *follow* you in the field, but should move ahead of your horse, changing direction at your will and returning at your command. To achieve this, without intimidation, is difficult. It requires discernment, patience and intelligence if it is to be accomplished, and the fine mettle and spirit of highly bred hounds preserved. But, it can be done, and is done. And few more beautiful sights are seen in this lovely world than a good man on a good horse with a well trained pack of foxhounds spread out in front of him.

So, let no one tell you that you waste your time when so occupied. If your other efforts insure the comfort and security of your family, and the prompt settlement of your debts, you can in no way be better employed than in devoting your leisure to schooling hounds.

Five pups are enough for one bitch to rear.

CHAPTER VII

BREEDING

Animal breeders are like prospectors, and grass widowers, confirmed optimists. Hound breeders and thoroughbred horse breeders are forever enthused about the possibilities of the next cross, and convinced that only the best qualities of sire and dam will be transmitted. Nothing can defeat this conviction, and men spend a lifetime making one breeding mistake after another.

There have been a few geniuses among hound breeders, and Kentucky has produced most of them. One stands out alone. Certainly in the last half century he has had no peers, and I doubt if, in any time or country, there has been his equal. No fox hunter reading this but already knows the man — Sam Wooldridge. The blood from his kennels flows through the veins of at least ninety per cent of all the good hounds in America. His contribution to the improvement of the Foxhound has been perhaps the greatest single influence in the sport.

The following rules are submitted in all humility. They represent chiefly the fruit of a lifetime of mistakes. I offer them somewhat in the spirit of a waiter I encountered long ago in Louisville. It was during Derby week, and at every restaurant where I had tried to get a table for breakfast, I had been rather impatiently refused. Finally, locating a cab driver's lunch counter and a vacant chair, I said to the waiter that all I wanted was two soft boiled eggs, — and some kind words. He nodded, soon reappeared with the eggs, set them in front of me, and then whispered in my ear, "Mistah, I wouldn't eat them eggs."

So I offer some "kind words" but use your own judgment upon these.

RULE 1. Use no hound for breeding that has a known fault. And be as sure as possible that there are no faults in the two preceding generations. Likewise be sure that the litter mate of the sire and dam you use are faultless.

RULE 2. Ruthlessly cull the unsuitable. Do this regardless of breeding, appearance or cost. Destroy the babblers.

RULE 3. Attend the National Field Trials. There you see the performance of the outstanding hounds of the country in competition. And you see the get of the leading stallion hounds on trial in the field.

RULE 4. The qualities of the sire and dam are what you may expect in their produce, so don't plan upon miracles. If you want nose, speed, and drive, be sure that *both* the sire and dam have them.

RULE 5. Don't look at your hounds with an "owner's eye." Be more critical of your own hounds than of any others.

I would furthermore suggest that if a hound isn't a creditable performer by the time he is eighteen months old, the best thing to do is to quit boarding him. Don't keep a boarder just to have more hounds. It is doubtful if any man ever owned a large pack of good hounds. If you can develop a small pack of really top hounds, well matched in speed, your name deserves to go down in sporting annals. Few men have bred and trained such a pack.

If I discussed Mendel's Law or expounded upon any of the known and established scientific principles of breeding, I would have to borrow somebody's word for them, so I shall, like an old friend I knew long ago in Wyoming, just try to be helpful from my own experience. My friend had a small ranch back where Indians and antelope were still more frequently seen than white men. In front of his log house was a "river" normally neither wide nor deep, and the commonly used trail forded at that point. I rode into the ford one evening with my mind blank, and only the fact that my horse could swim, and that I had simian prehensile instincts and hung to him, delayed my application for admittance at the Pearly Gates. Uncle Abe met me on the bank, in quite a sweat.

"Young fellar," he said, "I went to a lot of trouble to put that post in at the ford. And I cut a big notch in the post, which when hit air covered, shows hit haint fordable. What's the matter with you, — Kaint you read?" So, I in turn will cut a notch in a post, in the hopes that some later fellow traveler won't make the mistakes I have made.

There are no miracles in breeding. You mate animals with certain physical and mental characteristics, and the offspring show a blend of these same characteristics. If you want pups with nose, speed and drive, be sure that both the sire and dam have these qualities. And be just as sure that they have no faults. The first and most important job is to find a bitch that performs to suit you. Then, make sure that her sire and dam were outstanding performers, with no known vices. If you want your eye pleased, and who doesn't, — in addition to performance, she must have shape, and even the color you like. When you get such an animal, you are on your way to making a real success as a breeder of foxhounds. Your next job is to pick a sire. Fortunately, you don't have to own him, so picking the best is much simpler. But you should be careful, for every mistaken cross will greatly postpone your success. Here is where the Field Trials come to your aid. You can go to the National Trials and see many of the best hounds in America at work. And the Field Judges' decision upon them is of tremendous value. It is better than an individual's opinion. Nine good men, recommended by their State Associations, are chosen each year by the President of the National Fox Hunter's Association to act as Field Judges. These men are the cream of the foxhunting world, and whether one wears Texas spurs and hails from the border, or sits a "spring seat" saddle and hails from the mountains of Tennessee, you may be sure that he knows hound performance and will repeatedly risk his neck to impartially record virtues and faults. Some years ago while acting as M. F. H. at a National Trial, I found young Ed Walker who was a Field Judge, far from everybody, and down on the ground with his horse on top of him. When I came upon him, he had out his notebook and was scoring hounds with the calmness of a "home plate" judge.

To these "gentlemen unafraid," the correct information upon a performance of the moment by any one of two hundred hounds, justifies desperate chance taking. And when their scores are totaled, you may be assured that the best that could have been done has been achieved. Rarely, if ever, is one of these men a "city feller." Almost always they come from deep in the country where standards of honor and faith still make a high cult of sportsmanship. A recent example comes to my mind. At the National Trials in 1942, Eugene Torbett of Athens, Tennessee was one of the judges. A hound he had bred, but no longer owned, "Kentucky Buzzard," was entered in the All Age. To see that hound win the National would have meant more to "Gene" than anything in the world. The hound won, and became the National Champion. But when the scores were reckoned, "Gene" had turned in no score for him, — because he had bred him. Choose the sire from among the list that are high scored by the National Judges and you will have availed yourself of the best possible source of information. Now, having chosen the sire, you have done the best you can. In a year and a half, you will begin to find out whether or not the nick was a successful one. If it was not, you search for another, and so on . . .

No matter how good the grandsire and dam were, nor how many generations of the line you have bred, you must never breed from an individual that isn't what you want. Make no excuses for faults. I had a beautiful bitch some years ago that was all I could ask in performance, conformation, tongue and fox sense. When she was four years old, I began to hear her sling her tongue now and then when she entered a cover. I almost denied the discovery even to myself, and bred her to an outstanding hound. Half of her pups babbled and I eliminated them. The good ones I kept and bred. The next generation were all babblers, and I had to discard the whole bloodline. Even when the sire and dam are faultless, you may get pups that are not worth keeping.

Don't hesitate to look at the most beautiful hound you ever owned with the same critical eye with which you view your neighbor's hound. Does he run a covered track? Does he dwell? Admit faults and don't contest them with yourself. The Walker hound, I am told, owes much of its gameness to the fact that, when one of that great hunting family's hounds quit, he never left that field, but dangled forthwith by a halter from the nearest tree. Nothing, unless it's a red fox or a fighting cock, is as game as a good hound. That quality was developed because the quitters rarely lived to pass on the weakness. Successful animal breeders never deceive themselves, and they cull the unfit with a ruthless disregard for time or cost.

BROOD BITCHES: "Like begats like" is one old adage that Science has never refuted. If you plant burley tobacco, it will come up burley, — not one-sucker. The bitches you breed from should, as nearly as possible, represent what you want in a pack. Looking backward, I am amazed at the things I hoped to arrange in hound breeding. Subconsciously, I must have thought I was a god, for I tried to arrange miracles. One time, years ago, I had a little, shelly, light, and badly shaped bitch that was an outstanding foxhound. "A house afire in the woods," was the way an old blacksmith friend of mine used to describe her. I bred her to a rugged big boned hound exactly her opposite, with the idea that the pups would take her hunting qualities and their sire's conformation. There were six pups in the litter; two never equalled their dam in size and had the bone of a rat terrier; three were badly shaped but of good size, and one, the only really top hound among them, had a beautiful profile, but wasn't much thicker than a "Third Reader."

Width over loins is an important thing for a brood bitch. Then she must have whatever physical qualities you want in your pack. I have never been able to decide whether or not the dam was more important than the sire, but I am sure that the only way to get good foxhounds is to start with bitches that have no faults. Bitches in whelp should be fed twice a day, given as much milk as possible, and be allowed their freedom after the first month. Now comes a most important rule, one that represents the fruit of the experience of generations of great hound breeders:

Five pups are enough for one bitch to rear. You should take away the extra ones upon the fourth day after the milk demands of the larger litter have been made upon her. Five pups to a bitch means that the pups start life strong and healthy, and so are able to easily throw off disease later on. More than five mean that the whole litter is damaged. As soon as pups will lap milk, let them have it, preferably warm and fresh from the cow, — twice a day. This will relieve their mother and help them to grow. After they have lapped milk for two weeks, make up a thin oatmeal gruel and mix with the milk. Soon they will be swallowing the combination in fine fashion and you will have, one day, some beautiful hounds.

STALLION HOUNDS: If, as has been suggested, you choose the sire from the high scored list at the National, you insure quality to a considerable degree. Or, if you are qualified to judge such matters, select a hound which you have hunted many times and really know. But either selection is only a beginning, for the best hound mated to the best bitch will not be a guarantee of success. All you can do is to experiment until you get the right cross. When all the pups in a litter are good, you have probably solved your problems. But if one or two are mediocre, and the balance of the litter excellent, change the sire next time. If you were making watches, wagons or axes, you couldn't be satisfied if one out of five were not satisfactory.

The most wonderful individual may not transmit his qualities. Or he may, as is frequently the case, transmit them only to his daughters. So to insure success, you should select a stallion hound whose produce have proven him to be prepotent. And the State and National Field Trials do simplify this matter for you, since the get of many sires compete in these Trials.

It is a risky thing to use a young stallion hound, no matter how well he may be bred, nor how brilliant his work in the field. There may be weaknesses in his bloodlines that are slow about making themselves evident. Or he may develop faults that would be ruinous if carried on in the pack. It is true that most scientists agree that there is little chance of the transmission of acquired characteristics, but the weakness that caused the hound to acquire a fault may be transmitted. For example, a "thin skinned" hound may, in time, suffer so much from briars and thorns that he avoids them, and becomes a desultory hunter. Or a nervous hound may easily become a babbler later on, when he faces stiff competition. The four year old hound has demonstrated his virtues, and is obviously the safer sire.

Some families of hounds are brilliant in their first and second seasons, but lose ground rapidly thereafter and are worn out by the time they are five years old. Such lines are expensive to own. A hound is eighteen months old before it is really useful and it has cost a good deal to bring to that point. If it cannot continue to run up with the pack during its fifth and sixth years it isn't a good machine. Now and then you see hounds still in top form at seven and eight years. For example, "Puny Boy," owned by Justian Ellis of Tompkinsville, Kentucky, won the Tennessee All Age at Lebanon in his 6th year. I watched him closely during three hot days. Most of the casts were in "The Cedar Forest," a rocky rough country, full of briars, thorns and burrs. There were plenty of foxes and, although it was dry as dust, the running was excellent, — one slashing drive after another. We cast at dawn and the horn was never blown until three o'clock. "Puny Boy" was on top all the way and finished the three days fit as a fiddle. Such blood is of great value, for hounds that furnish two or three extra seasons of sport are worth a lot more than the equally brilliant ones that wear out just when they have reached a high level of usefulness. Sometime after the Lebanon hunt, I took a bitch to Tompkinsville to breed to "Puny Boy." Mr. Ellis is the County Agent there and has long been outstanding, not only in his profession but equally in his bird dogs and foxhounds as well. He told me that he travelled over a hundred miles to buy the hound and gave $150.00 for him at twelve months of age. It took great knowledge of pedigree to justify such a price for a pup, particularly since we don't overpay our county agents. But, it is such men who have so greatly contributed to hound breeding.

It takes a real hunting instinct to see the possibilities of a young hound. The greatest example of this I ever saw was years ago at a National Meet at Crab Orchard. "Big Stride" was running in the Futurity. W. K. Herrin of Clarksdale, Mississippi, had watched the young hound for two days, and when we were all gathered that night around the fire, he tried to buy the hound from his owner, Sam Wooldridge. But he made no progress. W. K. in those days kept a hundred hounds at Wartrace, Tennessee, and traveled up from the Delta to hunt them. And he knew a hound when he saw one. Wooldridge would always sell a hound. Like a jewel merchant, he had precious things, but would dispose of them. That night, however, he showed no interest. Cotton was high that year, and under such conditions the big Delta planters get what they want. Herrin bid and rebid, but Sam only tried to change the subject. Then Herrin took out his cheque book, wrote a cheque for one thousand dollars and handed it to Sam. There had never been a foxhound sold in America for such a price. Sam looked at the cheque and slowly tore it in two. The bare timeworn room in the old Crab Orchard Inn grew silent. For most of us, a thousand dollars was the kind of a sum that people got in a legacy, or at least for a crop of tobacco, and we were all aghast at seeing so much offered for a pup. I finally found my voice and pleaded with Sam to reconsider. He shook his head.

"This hound is worth more than that," he answered. "Anyhow, I am not going to sell him." How right both men were! "Big Stride" would have been a tremendous bargain at many times that price. No other animal perhaps ever left a greater imprint upon his species. It is almost impossible today to find a hound that does not trace back to him.

INBREEDING: Livestock breeders all insist that the only way to improve animals is to breed outstanding ones that are closely related (some even say the closer the better). From such an alliance will result an intensification of characteristics, and breeding on with the good ones, they, to a degree, insure that the resultant strain carries a heavy proportion of the desired qualities. I don't know about this. Cattlemen breed for shape. Thoroughbred breeders seek only speed, but hound breeders demand so many attributes that the problem is more difficult.

As a matter of fact, owing to the predominating influence of the Wooldridge kennels, most Walker hounds are closely related. Bob Lee Maddox once announced at our State Trials at Springfield that he had gone over into Carolina and bought a bitch that had no "Big Stride" blood in her. Everybody was tremendously interested in the phenomenon. I only discovered long afterwards that Bob was pulling our legs, — among highly bred hounds this would be distinctly an improbability.

A breeder will grow old attempting to make successful outcrosses, and such endeavors are only justifiable, in average cases, when you want an especial purpose hound. Otherwise, leave this task to the great breeders. It is the general conclusion of men with long experience that the same names should not appear in a pedigree sooner than the fourth generation but that beyond this a repetition of great names is likely to be of much value. Four crosses of "Flying Cloud" would be a good advertisement for any stallion hound.

BUYING HOUNDS

"An ass loaded with gold can pass through most doors," — but the kennel that houses a good pack has a very narrow one. Even wise and rich men find the *purchase* of a good pack of hounds to be a virtual impossibility. One really "top" hound is not easy to buy, — certainly you would grow gray trying to buy ten couple of the kind.

Look with suspicion upon the three or four year old hound offered for sale. Money will hardly buy a good hound of this age. If you are starting a pack, and know more than the rudiments of hunting, you may well buy year old hounds of good pedigree, with perhaps a few six-year old veterans to steady them, — and to find foxes. Your hunting will be ragged for a couple of seasons, but this is a better system than trying to buy a lot of good hounds and putting them together to form a pack. Lunsford Yondell almost furnished the exception that proved the rule. But he was a *foxhunter!* A better one never lived. And I doubt if anyone else could have ever made any kind of a pack in his way. He kept a hundred running hounds in his kennel, and after he left Kentucky and moved to Connecticut, he stopped breeding hounds and commenced a system of buying really top, seasoned ones. Lunsford had been born and reared in the middle of a hound country and was an outstanding judge of performance. He accepted the fact that a good three year old foxhound was worth a hundred dollars, and he was willing to pay even a higher price for a top one, — upon a trial basis. Appearance weighed very little in his scales, so long as the hound had the size, substance and general character of the pack. He bought few mediocre hounds and succeeded in maintaining one of the greatest packs ever assembled in this country. But no one else could have approached him in such an enterprise. He was like Sir Henry Morgan at the head of his pirates, — bold, resourceful, unorthodox, and determined to kill or be kissed. He could identify any hound's cry after hearing it once, which no other man I ever knew could do. This gift made it possible for him to hark his hounds to cry with unerring precision. The instant his ear caught the tongue of one of his dependables, he had the pack to him, on the line and away. The country he hunted was a cramped rocky and wooded one, but in those days, all stone walled. He followed his hounds over it like a hawk after gulls. No wall was too big for him to head a horse at and no jump blind enough to cause him to rein in. However, Lunsford Yondell won't happen anymore. He was left over from the days of Sir Francis Drake; and, if there is a Valhalla, has returned to it.

But even with his genius, the system of assembling good, seasoned individual hounds to make a pack wasn't quite satisfactory. Bold and brilliant the hounds were, but also inclined to jealousy, resentful of discipline. I believe that had he resided in a big, open grass country, he and his good huntsman, Charles Rankin, also a good hound judge and a masterful rider, might have welded together even under this system, the greatest fox catching machine of all time. But the Gods willed otherwise, and put them down in a rough country where one wooded tract joined another, and where even a winged horse would have had some trouble in following hounds.

The opposite method was used by my friend, Lowry Watkins, the great amateur rider, when he was assembling the "Oldham County Hounds." He wrote a number of Masters and suggested that they contribute old hounds. Everybody sent him a couple, and the result was I believe quite satisfactory. The pack perhaps didn't push a fox like Edmond Power's pack, nor like

Gist Finley's, but since it was largely made up of old hounds, it managed to give some good sport while he was breeding and training a young entry.

If I were starting a pack and were new at the game, I would pick out a foxhunter in whose judgment I had confidence and get him to help me select some foundation stock. If I were determined to start immediately, I would buy about three or more couple of aged hounds who were in their last season in a good pack, and then buy unentered young hounds of good breeding to go with them.

The registered "Walker" hound is, I am sure, an infinitely superior breed to the hounds normally found in organized packs. The better the horses the poorer the hounds, would be an almost certain rule. But the highly bred Walker hound that has been hunted mostly at night, or in the Trial fashion, is nearly useless to an organized pack. Few huntsmen can control him at all, and both his speed and range are too great for the hounds that cry with a broad "a." If Walker hounds are selected from tractable and sensible hound families and early entered with the pack, they may perform with great brilliance. But unless the pack becomes quickly standardized with this type of hound, it will be out of balance. The ordinary kennel bred packs have been bred, either by servants, or by men not primarily interested in hound breeding. And I doubt if even George Washington could have kept a pack of forty couples bred up to a creditable standard. These comments are not meant to be critical, for doubtless the heavier, slower hound, without great speed or zeal is frequently more useful for the purpose of giving business men a Saturday afternoon's relaxation. But for the lads whose coats are worn, and whose legs are long, — the sons of the "Long Hunters," those who hunt the Red Fox because bears and Indians are protected, for these gentlemen there is only one answer, — "the Walker hound with the Wooldridge Class." This type of hound is "thoroughbred" and is not easily managed by amateurs, nor by men accustomed to the more phlegmatic types. I am sure that if the foxes were asked for recommendations, they would warmly suggest that the sons of "Cork," "Big Stride," "Flying Cloud," and "Buzzard Wings," be ruled out.

There are few people who can have a happy time upon a thoroughbred in a hunting field. Most people should ride halfbreds. Likewise, I doubt if there are many men with the ability and time to develop and hunt a pack of these highly bred hounds. They will have more fun with something not so well bred, for such hounds are tractable, and generally don't run fast. Then too the type of hound should be suited to the country. In a suburban or limited country a pack of slow hounds doubtless would be more useful. They should be ideal for gentlemen who concern themselves with the *ritual* of sport. But for the Freemen, the boys who get down to serious hunting as soon as the crops move, only the best will serve.

The test of feed is how the hound feels.

CHAPTER VIII

FOOD

"What shall I feed my hounds?" asks every hunter in a half blinded search for Truth. But we turn our eyes from the nakedness of that slim lady. For we know that the question is not, what to feed hounds, but: "How shall I feed my hounds cheaply?"

Most everybody knows that a dog's food requirements are almost the same as a man's. In fact, the dog has been used in the major number of the experiments that have produced our nutritional discoveries. So the problem today is really an economic one, — we know what a dog *should* eat.

The unkenneled hound in a rich countryside will stay in good condition, for he keeps his diet in balance with rabbits, carrion, grasses and kitchen scraps.

But the hound that is kept kenneled has a difficult time in securing a balanced ration.

Cornmeal has long been the basic feed for hounds. My father's hounds were never fed anything but crackling cornbread. I presume that they and their kin a half century ago were expected, like the armies of those days to "live off the country." However, yellow cornmeal is still the cheapest and best base ingredient for hound feed. Neither a dog nor a man digests bran well. Nevertheless, it has real value in maintaining good elimination and should always be an ingredient of hound porridge. But, cornbread is the really valuable food. Left to himself, a negro eats cornbread, pork, turnipgreens and sorghum molasses. And his boys grow to be six feet tall, with broad shoulders and sound teeth. "He," a negro who helps with my hounds, won't eat any red meat but pork.

"Beef sticks in my teeth," he says. A comparison of vitamin values indicates that we have just learned what the Blacks found out long ago.

A hound's diet should include fat. Prepared feeds are always low in fat because it spoils quickly in storage. If you buy dry dog feed, add pork cracklings, mutton tallow or lard when you feed it. Cracklings keep well and are easily handled. I am never without them at the kennel cookhouse. They cost six or seven cents a pound year in and year out. Lard at fifteen cents per pound is not too costly an ingredient, for its value is more than three times that of the cereal in prepared feeds.

"Man cannot live by bread alone," was a line not written with a dietary view, but it is nevertheless true that bread is one of man's best foods, and contrary to the general idea, is an excellent one for dogs. Like man, the dog needs to supplement it with meat, but it furnishes a major portion of the required nutrients. Left over baker's bread is obtainable in most bakeries, can be bought cheaply, and is good for a hound. Dog feed companies buy it whenever possible.

A hound, like a man, handles starchy foods well. It never occurred to us to add potatoes to my hound feed, but in the war ravaged countries, potatoes are now a staple part of hound diet, and we are told that hounds utilize them well.

Oatmeal has long been the standby of hound feeders. Cooked just as it is cooked for people, it furnishes an excellent and inexpensive food. It generally sells in the feed stores at around $3.00 to $4.00 per hundred pounds. There is something in oats that produces nervous energy. Contrast the difference between a horse fed oats, with one fed corn. "Take away his oats," is the horseman's first advice for the control of a horse difficult to restrain. Meat is the natural base food for the dog, as well as for his cousins, the wolf and fox. And they all seem to thrive better upon raw than upon cooked meat. One trouble with the meat in prepared dog feeds is that it has been "cooked to death," and its vitamin values impaired. And to some extent, this appears to be true of canned dog meat. A sixty pound hound will live and prosper if fed nothing but three pounds of meat daily. He won't thrive upon any other single item of food. The best way to get meat for a pack is by using damaged horses and cows. Your veterinarian can help you solve this problem. Be sure to feed entrails and all the "innards" first. They have a vitamin and mineral content that will greatly contribute to your hounds' health and vigor. The way I do is to hang a carcass up on a gallows, disembowel it and call the pack to eat the entrails, etc. right there. By this method, much labor is saved.

Goats can, in ordinary years, be bought cheaply in Tennessee and no doubt in many other areas. A 65 pound goat generally sells for $2.00 and hounds will get forty pounds of food from such a carcass. For the man with a small pack, this offers an ideal source of protein in the right sized packages.

It is true that hounds can fill their protein requirements from plant sources as well as from meats. A dog digests 95% of his meat protein vs. about 60% from soybeans, or other plant sources. Peanut meal is a good meat substitute. Cottonseed meal seems to be a poison for dogs, although other animals use it well.

The vitamin needs of dogs are well known, since many of the vitamin discoveries were made using dogs in the dietary experiments. Their chief requirements are vitamins A - B - D — Niacin.

The sources from which they may get these are as follows:

A. — Liver, yellow plants such as carrots, cornmeal, tomatoes. Green colored alfalfa meal or chopped alfalfa is a good source of this vitamin; also cod-liver oil.

B. — Meat (particularly pork which is many times richer in this vitamin than beef), and oatmeal, brewer's yeast and wheat germ (whole wheat).

D. — Sunshine, cod-liver oil, irradiated yeast and milk.

Niacin — (This is the stuff that man must have in his diet to escape pellagra, or a hound have to escape black tongue). Meat, milk, eggs and leafy vegetables are the principal sources.

When it comes to saying just what a hound should be fed, the matter is, as was mentioned earlier, how to feed what the hound needs, at a low cost.

Here is a highly recommended dog feed formula now sold commercially:

Yellow cornmeal	35 parts
Bran	10 parts
Shorts	20 parts
Meat Scraps	10 parts
Fish Meal	10 parts
Dry skim milk or buttermilk	10 parts
Alfalfa Leaf Meal	2 parts
Bone Meal	2 parts
Salt	1 part
Sardine Oil	1 part

If you feed such a mixture four days a week, and feed meat the other three, your hounds would do well. The main thing to remember is meat, and the next thing is leafy vegetables. If these are included in your hound feed, the chances are that you won't go far wrong.

Start the little puppies to lapping warm cow's milk when they are three weeks old. Stick their noses in the pan and they will soon be going for it in earnest. At five weeks, give them ground meat, and try to have them eating everything at two months. A good start is half the race, and if your hounds are richly fed for the first six months, most later problems are conquered.

There is no magic about feeding man or beast. If you try to feed either cheaply, you will invite trouble. The answer about hounds is not to keep more than you can afford to properly feed.

If their feed consists of some such mixture as the following, it seems to me that your hounds will do well most of the time.

Oatmeal	20 Parts
Cornmeal	30 Parts
Fresh Meat	30 Parts

(Pork Cracklings to be substituted when out of meat, but fresh meat should be fed twice a week).

Shorts	5 Parts
Bran	5 Parts
Salt	1 Part
Alfalfa Leaf Meal	2 Parts

(Must be green, not brown in color. I prefer to cut a bucket of green alfalfa in the field instead of using the meal).

Bone Meal	2 Parts
Milk	5 Parts

But fresh vegetables should be added to this diet. Use potatoes instead of oatmeal occasionally, and when greens, turnips, carrots, etc., are available, cook them with the meat. Feed tomatoes when they are cheap, or tomato pomace at other times.

The test of feed is how the hound feels and looks that eats it. If he is full of life, and his hair is glossy, then he and his feed agree. But he must also have energy and show it. When a hound is turned out of the kennel, he should bound up and down like a Jack-in-the-box, and should tumble about like a boy just out of school. Of course, to act this way, the hound must be free of parasites. Hounds that crawl out from under the house like a town negro going into a hay harvest, are generally full of worms. Until hounds are worm free, good feeding, like steamboat whiskey, is more productive of hope than happiness.

COOKING

To begin, fill your kettle with water and let it come to a boil. Then, put in the block of cracklings (first chopping it into small pieces). When these have boiled twenty to thirty minutes, pour in the oatmeal, together with a large handful of salt, and stir steadily so that none may stick to the bottom or sides of the kettle. A straight hoe, of the kind used for edging, makes the best thing for this purpose. With the hoe, it is easy to keep the food from sticking.

When the oatmeal has boiled about five minutes, put in the cornmeal, and continue stirring. When this is cooked, which takes six to ten minutes, add the bran, and stir two or three minutes. Then draw the fire. Now, after a quarter of an hour, with a long handled shovel, dip the pudding into the feed troughs and leave it several hours to cool. Or, if you want to make one cooking do for several days, turn each shovelful down separately upon a large table top and the pats will cool into loaflike consistency.

If you have meat on hand, it, of course, takes the place of cracklings. It may be either boiled with the pudding, or fed fresh.

Baking the feed takes perhaps more time, but has many advantages, since it can be handled and carefully distributed. The harder it is baked, the better, as this condition forces the hound to chew it up, and prevents his bolting it. If your oven is large enough, you can bake several days supply at a time. In fly season, this is very useful. There are perhaps some commercial dog foods better than others, but none that will keep a running pack of hounds in fit condition unless supplemented by meat. Such feeds are expensive and fed alone not too valuable, but provide a way to feed a small pack with a minimum of work.

Many men will not spend money to properly feed their hounds, and refer to the gaunt, woeful looking, slat-ribbed wrecks, that crawl out from under the house when a stranger rides up, as being "in running shape." Thirty-odd years ago, trotting horses were conditioned upon the "accordion ribbed" plan. And, to insure their condition, were sweated under blankets between heats. However, no one is left in the world, but the occasional fox hunter, who believes that athletes are conditioned upon a siege diet. Oddly enough, there are many prominent hunters of the older generation who know all about balanced rations for cattle, but think that a hound can live upon manna from Heaven. If you hunt hounds, you are supposed to see that their ribs are kept covered. Those who can't afford, or haven't time, to feed properly, should not keep a pack of hounds.

Dogs are used in hospitals more than any other animal to test the effects of foods and medicines upon man. So if you get to wondering about what your hounds should eat, just remember that their needs are very much like your own, except that they need about twice the protein ratio that you require. The hound raised at your kitchen door will do better than any kennel fed one, because he will get a better balanced diet.

Many hounds are so well bred, that although near starvation, they will run a fox until they drop. When you see a hound whose hip points show, starvation is at work. His owner will say "running shape." Tell him the truth, in the interests of sportsmanship, — and fight your way home, if you must. Your hounds should be fed as carefully as your cattle are, for a properly fed good hound will put a badly fed hound's "feet to the fire" every time. Energy, like steam, is produced by fuel. If you want hounds that can "stay in the race," and take punishment, just remember that plenty of good food is the answer. Fresh meat must be fed at least once a week. If you are sure of the health of the animal slaughtered, feed the meat raw, at least upon alternate occasions. But don't feed raw pork.

As mentioned at the beginning of this chapter, within a radius of six or seven miles of your kennel a horse, mule or cow is damaged, or dies of accident, every week. If through advertising in the county paper or other means, you let it be known that you will dispose of such animals, you can get them for the hauling. A horse hide brings from two to five dollars and if you give this hide money to your men, they will butcher these animals with pleasure. Of course, when summer comes, unless you have refrigeration, you cannot use this source of meat. But during the hunting season, it is an ideal way to provide hounds with their protein requirements.

Milk is, of course, excellent for hounds. Even skimmed milk or buttermilk contributes valuable elements and should be added to their feed whenever available.

The best rule is to feed generously, and then try to keep hounds in condition by plenty of work. A hound, like a horse, must have exercise if he is to race.

As soon as a pup will lap cow's milk, it should be provided. There is absolutely no scientific basis for the prevalent belief that cow's milk brings worms. For that matter, worms are present in all pups. After a week or two of supplementing the diet with cow's milk, start adding a little cooked oatmeal, enough to make a thin gruel. Then at two months, begin to feed small portions of fresh, ground meat. Feed the pups four times a day until four or five months old, then three times up to six months, and after that, until a year old, twice a day.

If you have a highly bred litter, whose growth and development you are determined to insure, feed them at from one to three months everything a six months old baby eats, and from four weeks on, add small daily amounts of finely ground meat, of course increasing it as they grow older. They should be fed three times a day until four months old, and at least twice a day then until grown.

For bitches in whelp, save the table scraps. A mixed diet that includes meat, vegetables and cornbread is ideal. The lactating bitch must be generously fed upon a well balanced diet of meat, vegetables, cereals and milk. In relation to her size, she produces milk as well as a good cow, but to do so, she must have both abundance and quality of food. And for her and her pups, you must not forget cod-liver oil.

Shade, water and drainage.

CHAPTER IX

THE KENNEL

The man who keeps five or six hounds generally doesn't need a kennel, for the hounds do well enough scratching their fleas under the appletree or the children's bed. In fact, they do much better. But, six hounds are as many as most wives will tolerate, at least without daily comment. So, a kennel eventually seems necessary. Its location is, of course, generally governed more by necessity than choice. It should, however, face North so that the yards will be on the South. Really, it would be best on top of a hill to insure good drainage, and it should have a spring bubbling through it. But, alas, only Empyrean springs bubble out of hilltops, so it is frequently necessary to compromise. But running water is a tremendous asset to a kennel, almost a necessity. If you can't locate near the spring, pipe water to the yards and cookroom. Or drill a well, for you must have plenty of water. It should be under pressure, so the concrete floors can be hosed off, — for in a kennel as in a kitchen, dirt means death. Good drainage is very important. The South slopes of hills are excellent kennel locations. If the kennel yards have shade, water and drainage, they meet requirements. A yard which included a cave would doubtless be perfect for our hot summers. Rock ledges have a decided usefulness in the yards and so has a gravel soil.

Of late years people have begun to use wire for kennel yards. This is not only expensive but often impractical. The cheapest and best material is hardwood "stacking staves." Wherever lumber has been stacked you can buy these at from 2 to 5 cents each. They are approximately 1 x 3 inches and should be cut off at eight feet. The cracks should be three inches apart. One hound in fifty may at times get out of this fence, but if the posts and stringers are put on the outside, none will. Such a fence can be completed, and perhaps painted, for much less than wire. If the staves are chestnut or oak (as they frequently are), the posts seasoned black locust, and the stringers cypress, chestnut, or white oak, the fence (if painted upon the years that you get a good price for tobacco) will hold hounds for your grandson. Around the base of the fence, and, of course, inside the enclosure, bury old woven wire fencing, so that the hounds can't scratch underneath.

The kennel yards should be divided four ways: two yards for dogs, three for bitches, one for special use (cripples, visitors, etc.) and a large grass yard to turn out in when the other yards are being cleaned, or upon similar occasions. An additional small yard for quarrelsome hounds is very useful.

The more space you give a hound, the healthier he is, so the large grass yard should be as extensive as your purse or situation will permit. The other yards should have as much as 200 square feet to the hound; i. e. for a ten-hound yard, a minimum of forty by fifty feet. All the yards should have shade, and, if possible, fresh water.

The cookroom can be simplicity itself: a fireplace, with a crane to hang a waterbucket on, provides warmth as well as hot water when you need it. Then a 30-inch kettle(for 20-30 hounds) set in stone or brick, and at the side of it an oven of the same material.

To store your oatmeal, cornmeal, etc., cut out the tops of alcohol or oil drums, and have the tinner make metal tops with handles. Or perhaps better still have them made of copper screening. This arrangement will keep the rat population down, and save you a great deal of expense. Cracklings are more difficult to store since circulation of air is required and several months' supply must be kept on hand. But any dry, ratproof container which permits the free movement of air around the cracklings will prove satisfactory.

The feed yard should have a minimum area of ten square feet to the hound, but fifteen square feet is better. For ten couples of hounds, a space 15 x 20 feet is enough. The pavement should be of smooth finished concrete. In fact, it should be a slick surface, so that food, offal, etc., will wash right off of it. The pavement should slope to a central drain connected to a six inch tile, pitched sharply enough so that when you hose the yard no drainage problems can bother. If you have "town money" and live North of Tennessee, a corner of the yard had well be sheltered and roofed. If you have piped water, one hydrant should be in the food yard, which must be hosed out and scrubbed daily after feeding.

The best feed troughs are made by cutting old galvanized kitchen hot water tanks in two pieces lengthwise. This provides a durable, rustproof and easily cleaned up trough. Two of these will adequately feed twenty couples, although three makes the feeding more convenient. And you should have a couple of small troughs as well.

The housing of hounds is of course dictated by climate, for obviously, Michigan and Tennessee have different conditions to meet. South of the Mason and Dixon line, the best lodging rooms I have seen have been whiskey barrels. With one to a hound, they provide seclusion, warmth and shelter, in a rather perfect way. Small shelters with hinged or removable roofs, are much better than the conventional kennel houses, for they can be thrown open to the sun upon bright days.

The best kennel design, is a circular one with the yards shaped like slices of pie, and all opening into an inner circle containing the kitchen, etc. The lodging rooms should all be built around the inner circle, one to a yard, and should have doors opening on this circle, so that removing the litter can be easily done. At the side of each lodging room, there should be a small yard as well, perhaps 6 x 12 with gates at the ends, so that hounds may be drafted from them with greater ease. If a rectangular design is used, all yards should open upon an aisle which in turn should lead both to the feed lot and also to the small yard where hounds are selected for the working pack of the day.

Let them work the ground with care.

CHAPTER X

HUNTING

How do you hunt a fox? Some say that you get on your horse, blow your horn, jog out to "The Knobs," and hiss your hounds into the woods. Others say that you first go up to Lexington and buy yourself a seventeen hand thoroughbred horse; then you order some boots, some coats, etc., and go looking for fences. "Maybe they is two ways to look at this," as the Parson said when he was caught in the hen house. However, if you want to do a real job of foxhunting there is one thing you must have, and that is a pack of honest hounds, well matched in speed and temperament. Oddly enough, it seems that you can't *buy* a pack of good hounds. At least, no one has thus far been able to do this. There may be one exception to the rule, but generally speaking, those that have top horses have bottom hounds. And you can't hire anybody to breed a pack of good hounds for you. A man with that much sense wouldn't work for anybody else. A rich man can have a wonderful stable of horses, because he can hire any amount of men who can both buy them and breed them. But there are no hired hands capable of breeding and developing a pack of real working foxhounds. So, if you want to hunt a fox, you must first breed a pack.

It is not much fun to fox hunt unless your hounds are trained as a pack. That means, unless they will respond to your horn and voice, hark readily to cry and run as a team, instead of jealous individuals. Really well bred hounds are not much trouble to break to fox. A couple of good runs and such hounds are interested in little else. However, now and then you may have difficulties. An occasional hound is rabbit crazy and, beat him as you will, is never altogether steady. Don't waste too much time upon such hounds, nor upon the bloodlines that produce them. Hounds that have the right blood rarely run riot.

I have had hounds leave a running fox for a rabbit. Surely there is no greater descent into degradation. Nevertheless, many hounds will, upon bad scenting days, give a cat, a cur dog, or anything else that moves, a short burst. The thong is the answer for this; and if poured on liberally, you won't have to serve this tea so soon again.

Few hounds ever make top "fox dogs" unless they start out life with some brilliance. If they stand around and don't want to hunt, and then go in and out of a race, the chances are that they will not make good hounds. Now and then such a hound will make a fair one in his second year, but I have never seen these slow starters develop into anything beyond second raters. Years ago someone gave me a young "gyp" that made no effort to hunt the first season. In the second season, she became an active, useful hunter, although not outstanding. I have clung on to many hounds since, hoping that they would do likewise. None have. Conversely, hounds that start well rarely turn out badly. Now and then one may develop a vice, such as running cur dogs, or barking at livestock, but generally he is so absorbed in the game of running a fox that little else will ever interest him.

A hound should not be started upon the Red Fox until he is fully matured; fourteen months is soon enough. Even then, he will not profit by the wear and tear of hard running such as he is apt to get in a fast pack. A long hard run after a January fox takes a lot out of any hound. If left alone afterwards, they will sleep the clock around, come out to eat and then curl up for more rest. This pull upon heart, nerve and sinew is too much for any but the unusual young hound. But, after eighteen months, the youngsters "take the gaff" without great distress, and six months later are as tough as shoe leather and eager for the punishment of long races.

"Hill Toppers" attach more importance to courage in a hound than they do to nose or any other quality. The hound that quits in these night "races" brings opprobrium down upon his owner's pate. But there is here something of the synthesis that so frequently transforms the onlooker at all sports. No one is so critical of speed as a fat man at a football game. But the old athlete is not so much inclined to demand the immediate execution of the failing runner. And the man who *follows* hounds understands a little better the relation between pluck and condition. I have little patience with the man who rides the lanes (either in a saddle or a car) and is critical of "heart" in a hound. We have all seen men with only one leg ride like blazes across country. I knew one man long ago who had lost both legs, yet had himself strapped to the saddle and saw most of the fun. Such a man's criticism of a hound's courage might be entitled to full consideration.

Turning a pack of hounds loose in a big woods and sitting by while hounds either find a fox, or, failing, go off in the adjoining county and look for one, has always seemed to me a pastime better suited for raconteurs than hunters. Directing an orchestra must be more interesting than listening to one. Even umpiring a ball game is more sport than just watching it. Actively hunting a pack is one of the most stimulating and fascinating things the poor "homo sapiens" ever found out about. But, to hunt a pack, you first must have one; then train it, and lastly know how to direct its activities. No bird hunter would just *follow* his bird dog around, yet how many foxhunters are quite willing, once the craft is launched, to let wind, tide, and Destiny, indicate the course.

You first must be able to take your pack to the place of meeting. Then, if that Fox isn't at home, you must be able, with reasonable celerity, to assemble it and go to another place where a fox lives. The alternative is going where your hounds decide to go, which frequently would be where you couldn't. If breeding, feeding and training have received adequate attention, the control of hounds in the field follows as a natural corallary — provided you are a hunter.

When a rider is afraid, the horse knows it sooner than the man does. Likewise, when a man isn't a hunter, a hound quickly understands it, and goes independently on his way thereafter. "When in doubt, do nothing," is a sound guide. A few misdirections and hounds will be as indifferent to you as to a babbler. But, contrawise, set them forward on the line now and again, or hark them to the faint cry of old "Longstreet" over the hill, and your place is assured. Of course, you must continue to merit their respect, for a hound listens neither to brother nor to Master whose voice is not a frequent assurance of better things. Hunting hounds is like calling a square dance, you must know what you are doing, — and know the calls as well.

THE FIND: We all agree with Mr. Addison that "hunting is not a proper employment for a thinking man," but, if the old head will clear up occasionally, we can be of great help to hounds. Remember that you, high up on a horse, have a much greater field of vision, — even if your scenting qualities, like ours, are a little dulled by having had your nose in a bottle, or over a pipe, for many years. Say, for example, that hounds are working upon a stale potato kind of a line and "getting nowhere fast." You see the "Red Ranger" steal away across a distant field of emerald wheat, and hasten to put them on the line. When they inhale that fresh intoxicating scent, they are sold upon your ability. And the next time they will fly to you.

When you approach the woodland where Mr. Fox lives, your hounds should be in front of you. At fifty to one hundred yards distance, stop your horse and give the signal that sets the pack free to begin the search. Always use the same words upon these occasions. "Leu in, leu in" . . . is the time honored command, but many others are used. However, "leu" doesn't sound like anything else and therefore has a great advantage. Whatever you say, never change the command.

The distance at which you stop from the woods should vary with their size, for you want hounds spread over a wide front when they enter the cover. Many a fox is bypassed when hounds first go in, and lies snug until the whole parade has gone on, then quietly steals away back over the line of your approach. Of course, more foxes steal out of small woods in advance of the entry of the hounds. In a large woods, the problem is reversed; it is not how to prevent Br'er Fox stealing out, — but how to drive him out that concerns you.

Since we first must find our fox, we must have hounds that will spread wide and draw well. Spread is the width of ground that your hounds cover in front of you. This varies, of course, with the country, but on the average may be something near a half mile; that is, the pack is moving through the country in a skirmish line of about that width. If they attempt to cover a more extensive front, they are apt to get away on the line individually, rather than collectively. However, bold Reynard rarely bursts into the open like a fire horse. Generally, he circles a time or two through the woods before he is pushed out, and during these swings scattered hounds hear the cry and hark to it.

As a basic rule, the better bred the hound the wider he hunts. And, unless you hunt some paradise of small covers and big fields, the wide hunting hound is necessary. But here again, we must be careful about terms. To a Field Trial hound breeder, a wide hunting hound is one that thinks nothing of ranging miles away in search of a fox. Some, in fact are encouraged to just "keep going" until they find a fox. After the National was run at Bowling Green, one bitch was picked up a week later about sixty miles north, and she was hunting hard when found. A hound like that is not very useful if you want a coordinated pack of hounds that will get away together with a fox. But some of the blood may be of great value. Many of these inbred field trial hounds are timid, wild, and difficult to handle. They are like thoroughbred horses in that they can outperform any other type. But they are too individualistic for team work. There are, however, some level headed families that are susceptible to training, and a pack of this kind cannot be equalled, or even approached, by any other hounds upon earth. However, for the man who is not predominantly interested in hounds, some of the slower and more phlegmatic breeds, either the imported, or the type sometimes bred along our Eastern shores may be more useful. And the country has much to do with the kind of hounds you should use. If it is open with big fields and with few obstacles that are apt to long delay a vigorous horseman, then there is a possibility that the "Buzzard Wings" type of bloodstock may be considered, — if you have patience, time and a way with hounds. But in a lesser country, and particularly if you are not bred and born a "hound man," the slower kinds are apt to be more useful.

When the scenting is good, hounds hunt without any need for assistance, but upon a bad scenting day, they require some direction, and if the sun is warm but the ground still chilled, then you have but one chance, and that is to steal up close to old Red and flush him out of cover as a cur dog jumps a rabbit. Then, your job is to keep your hounds in motion, and to cover as much ground as possible. For upon such days, when you stop, within a few minutes hounds begin to drift towards you, and to stand in silent contemplation of anyone so dumb as to hunt when there is no scent. So keep your horse moving slowly at such times, or your hounds may stand still. You must cover a lot of ground if you expect to flush a fox. If he steals away ten minutes in front of you he will leave so little scent upon these days that it may be useless to follow. Your chance is to jump him, and then to push him hard. If hounds let him amble away, they will never run him. He must be forced to fly, if the pack is to be able to follow with any success. So this is the time to hunt quietly, to encourage hounds to spread like skirmishers and to draw with care. Upon such days, many foxes like to sun themselves upon a south slope in a sedgegrass field, particularly if the field be close to a woodland. Nor upon these occasions must you pass up any thick cover where a fox may lurk. Keep trying, and, as the afternoon lengthens your chances improve. By four o'clock, even upon a bad day, things will be better.

It is possible to jump a fox, of course, upon any day, but there are days when hounds simply cannot run one a hundred yards. When you take hounds out upon such times, it is like going to a wedding when you have had advance information that the bride will not appear. People ride gaily along in the sunshine and chatter that, "its almost like a May day." Only you and the hounds know the doleful facts, and, like crows at a hog killing, you wait until the funeral aspect of the situation becomes apparent before you commence your doeful dirge about difficulties.

"Bad scenting day," is, of course, the huntsman's alibi for all the failures of pedigree, of method, and of ignorance. And since most days are bad, just as most nights are good, the huntsman is not lying when he groans, "It will be a tough job to run a fox today." The answer is to have a wonderful pack of hounds. If you want to run a fox at times convenient to yourself, you must have a pack with really good noses. And too, it must be made up of hounds that get forward with a line. The hound that sniffles at the hummocks and tries to work slowly, upon bad scenting days will stay too far behind a fox too long to be able to unravel the thread of scent. To push a fox, then, your pack must at every check swing in great arcs and try to get forward. Now a Field Trial type worker is useful, one that swings far ahead to intercept the line. For to stay with the fox upon such a day, hounds must not linger over mysteries. Instead, they must almost guess the line of the fox, and keep pressing forward to recover the loss. Upon good scenting days hounds do better if they are more patient with the line. By this, I mean if they don't try to gamble. But upon the bad days they must shoot the dice, "to win, or lose it all."

Always when your hounds find the fox it is highly important that he be promptly pushed. Minutes saved at the start mean the difference between a good run and a poor one. If your hounds "boo-hoo" around the woods, trying to puzzle out the line inch by inch, old Br'er Fox slips quietly away on the other side, and has a mile or two of comfortable lead before the pack decides which way he went. But if they hit his outgoing line well packed up, they will have a fresh and pungent scent to follow, and he will have to go away straight and make a run for it. Among your hounds will be an old warrior who knows all about this, and he will be circling the edges of the cover to find the foxes exit line. Amid the woodland cry you hear his voice on the other side. You listen a few seconds to make sure he is right and then that way you plunge, harking your hounds to him. Let the woods ring now with your, "Hark to Lowry," for these are the seconds that count most of all. The ancients, and traditionalists, want to pop whips, or to beat upon their boots at this juncture, in order to bestir the laggards and to get them forward upon the line. Perhaps they are right? Certainly the pack must get away together if we are to drive this fox with dash and style. But it should be enough that hounds either hear the leaders leaving, or hear the excitement of your voice. If any thereafter hang around the woods, have a look at their pedigrees, for you may have to change your breeding stock. The cry of an honest hound taking a fox out of a woodland should electrify his brethren, and if they are good foxhounds of his own pack they should need no threats to hasten them to him, but should go as fast as ever they can put their feet to the ground, and without any compulsion whatsoever.

In the days when Wooldridge and "Big Stride" were hunting the Woodford County hills together, it was worth a hundred mile trip to watch the pair run a fox. Into a woods would go the pack and quickly out of it would come that King of Hounds, his matchless tongue saying with perfect clarity "this is the way he went." And then Wooldridge would stand in his stirrups and call:

"Hark to Big Stride! Hark to the Big 'Un!" would sweep those other great hounds, Ch. "Cleo," Ch. "Pride," "Long Run," "Heepman," . . . and thirty more almost as good, into a pack at once, and away they would sail after the fox like eagles in flight. There was something in Sam Wooldridge's voice, some stavistic vibrancy that set a hound forward as though shot from a bow. You and I can't be Carusos or Wooldridges, but if we hark hounds forward with all the voice we have at this critical time, we will do a lot to make that run a good one.

Now we are away and the pack is skimming a great wheatfield like a distant sail upon green water. To our ears floats the mad cry, that barbaric music that, like the bagpipes in the Highlands, frees the listener of caution, care and memory, and stirs him madly forward. Ten minutes of this and we would never catch them, — but then we encounter . . . CHECKS, LOSSES AND BOTHERS.

One man says, "hounds have checked," and the next one says "they have made a loss," and the third says, "made a bother." It doesn't make any difference. Words may be "the storied treasures of the tomb in which the ages lie," but you could hunt a fox in Italian, I daresay. The difference between a check and a loss is a matter of degree. The check is short, a brief interruption, whilst the loss is either of longer duration, or a permanent affair. Even then the use of these descriptive terms is somewhat a matter of who is speaking. The "bother" is a wonderfully descriptive term and has largely replaced "check." It exactly describes the usual interruptions and carries a connotation of mental reaction to them.

In a nearby hill county there is an area in which the matter of subsistence must have at one time been of some concern, for one post office is named "Lick-skillet," and the "Empty Gut Road" is an artery of importance. The inhabitants of the region are not easily bowed by the winds of mischance, and stubbornly refuse to admit misfortune. An old friend of mine hunts part of the area, with the help of eight long eared hounds and a longer eared mule. I came upon him one day sitting upon his mule in a lane watching his hounds work up and down a fence row. When I inquired if he had lost his fox, he stroked his long beard and shook his head.

"No, we hain't exactly lost him, — but the hounds bin off his trail for an hour or two."

There are a thousand variations of checks and losses. And there are two entirely different schools of thought about what a man hunting hounds should do upon these occasions. The men who have their breeches made in New York are uniformly of the opinion that, upon these occasions, you should gallop the pack about in concentric circles, in an organized effort to "hit it off." The men who know the breeding of their hounds, don't agree with this method, but believe that you should sit still, and let the hounds solve these problems. Ordinarily the pedigree school is right. Most of the time the problem is a hound's responsibility. However, there are many times when the huntsman can be helpful after hounds falter, and fail to get on with the run. But the chief way to be useful is to keep your eyes and ears concerned with the activities of the best of your older hounds. And when you hear a whimper from one of them or see him feathering across the plough, move slowly after him, so, if he hits it off you are in the right position to get hounds to him. Losses are not always ended by a pealing of church bells. Frequently, the hound that determines the way old Br'er Fox went out is diffident about his own decision, and anxious to have a running line again before he boasts of victory, so he cries but faintly, whimpers over the doubtful places and feathers along the worst. The other hounds frequently don't hear any of this, so you may speed the hunt up in great fashion if you watch your old, tried and true hounds and hark the pack to them when they recover a lost line. "This looks simple," as the cook said when he sighted the sextant. And so it is, if you know the true worth and value of each of your hounds in any hunting situation. But such knowledge can be neither gained from this nor any other book. You really must "know where the wild thyme grows" if you are to know the ways of hounds and foxes.

To illustrate for the neophyte a simple "loss:" Ahead the sound suddenly ceases, and when we gallop up, hounds are scattered widely, some working towards thirty acres of woodland to the right and the remainder fanned out in a widening semi-circle, sterns swishing, noses down, trying desperately to straighten out the line. It is not too good scenting, and sun's rays grow steadily warmer. Ten minutes more and we may never push our fox again this day! What's the answer? Just then, half a mile away, to the right rear, you glimpse old "Mischief," nose to the ground, working across a piece of plough land. He isn't saying anything, but long observation has taught you that this hound has a way that can be trusted upon these occasions, and you trot towards him, listening. He reaches a patch of sedgegrass and cries once, then again! The hounds ahead in the valley can't hear this. Already some of them are almost out of sight. You turn your horse's head, double on your horn, and, starting for "Mischief," raise the echoes with:

"Hark! Hark to Mischief!" Back from the valley, out of the wood, they scramble. Now they catch the distinct cry and are away to it. Three — four minutes, and the roar of the pack is in your ears. The race is on again. Now, you didn't bother them when they were at loss. You sat still, watched and listened. And when the right moment came, you helped them. They shan't soon forget it. They are a better working pack for it. Sam Wooldridge's *voice* has gone a long way to develop champions. And yours, in turn, used at the right time, will do likewise. At a loss, you must first be quiet, then look, and listen. If the pack needs your help, be sure they get it. When the next check comes, it is, we will say, well into a vast expanse of sticky ploughed fields. In vain the hounds circle and try. The sun is hot, the ground cold; ten minutes pass. Your judgment tells you that "Time is on the wing," and the fox is lost unless the line is soon recovered. Far ahead is pasture land. You noticed colts galloping across it perhaps when hounds first checked. What should you do? Tap your horn a couple of times and gallop towards the grassland with your hounds. Well into it, bring your horse to a walk. Watch the hounds now get their noses down, circle and try for the line! No luck! Then ahead you see "Beauty" stern swishing, trying to "own" something. Hounds cross and recross around her, but none get a message. If she wavers now, give her your whispered assurance and support:

"Try him — Good girl — try him!" And then she whimpers, presses forward, and speaks! The pack flies to her, noses down. One catches it! Another! They honor a good bitch with a roar of cry and are away again.

To hunt a pack of fox hounds means to *help* them. To do that, you must know a lot about a fox, and about scent. And you must know your hounds, their weakness, strength, and peculiarities. You must know which ones to watch at certain times, when to chide, when to encourage, and when to be silent. The more you have rabbit hunted, coon hunted, shot over bird-dogs, acquainted yourself with the out of doors, and the ways of wild life, so much the better fox hunter you will be. For the pursuit of a fox is *hunting,* and shares with the pursuit of all wild game certain of woodcraft and hunting instinct. If you are a city bred fellow, don't try to hunt a pack of hounds. Only a countryman can ever master the game. Sometimes I wonder if it can be really mastered by any other than a man bred to it. The city man cannot get out of his head a conviction that fox hunting is just a horse game, closely akin to racing.

If you are just starting with a pack, be sure that your hounds represent more value than your horses. Otherwise, you are forever branded by real fox hunters as a "captain of industry." Don't build a fine stable and use a chicken yard for a kennel. Build a decent kennel, and shelter your horses under a strawstack if you must. For unless you have good hounds and train them well, all your efforts to do a real job at hunting a pack will like wind in the woods, move more leaves than oak trees.

A good hunting hound is like a good bird dog, in that first he must have nose, and secondly he must have an idea where to look for his game. The "busy" hound, that sticks his nose into every grass clump and stick pile, and dashes about with his tail oscillating like the clapper in a bell, rarely finds foxes. Foxes, like criminals, are found by those who know where to look for them, and years ago, while serving as M. F. H. for the National when we hunted in Madison County, Kentucky, I had a clear illustration of this. Of course, there are more good fox hunters in that County than there are in Heaven. Even the Blacks are organized and have, or had, the "Madison County Negro Fox Hunters Association." I was very anxious to have the first Meet where we were sure to find a fox, so I went to the fine old negro who headed that Association and asked him where I should cast hounds. He "gave me the scripture," book, page and verse. I cast where he said, in two acres of sedge and brambles, and out popped a fox in full view of everybody. Hounds ran him a long way and finally brought him back and rolled him over within two hundred yards of a thousand spectators. Many people thought it was a bag fox, but it was not. The run was made possible only because a sagacious old Negro knew where his fox friends stayed.

So a hound that can find foxes, — a good "strike dog," — is a valuable asset to the Pack. But if, after finding, he doddles about and dwells on the line without getting forward, he should find a new home. That kind do you as much harm as good. A "strike dog" that can find the fox and hustle him out is what you want. Your pack should be liberally filled with these, and not dependent upon one or two hounds to do the work. When you begin to notice that one hound makes most of your finds, leave him at home for a while and break the pack of the habit of depending upon him. Obviously the ideal pack would be composed of hounds that were good at finding as well as at running a fox.

No man is a good hunter unless he knows where to look for his game, so *you* share much of the responsibility for finding a fox. Even in a country like Middle Tennessee, where foxes are very numerous, you have to take your pack to where Br'er Fox lives if you want to run. And you have to know just which wood is his frontyard, and in which sedgefield he is wont to sun himself.

Suppose you have moved your hounds to a strange country. How do you find out where the foxes live? If there is a foxhunter in residence, you ask him, and he will tell you where every fox in his nighborhood dens, how many cubs each vixen reared, and where to go to "hit him." If there is no foxhunter, ask the coon hunters or the squirrel hunters. And failing these, ask the farm boys. These lads who go to the back pasture to salt the steers, or up the hill after the sheep, are the ones who see foxes. Just at sunup, they meet his Royal Highness. On the edge of a wood perhaps, as the morning mists dissolve, the Red Ranger with the inscrutable eyes meets them and disappears so fast that memory overtakes vision. Or at night, driving the stray heifer home, a shape like a wraith disputes the pathway for an instant, and makes an evening's adventure. Negroes see foxes. Both do some silent night prowling on similar missions and there is kinship and competition in their contacts. Don't question storekeepers, preachers or prosperous farmers, for they never know anything but prices, sins and pedigrees. To know where foxes live you must also know where the wild bee stores honey, the tree where the white owls live, and a lot of other things that are neither written in books nor chanted in the market-place.

Most hunters know, reasonably well, the individual cry of their hounds. When a hound opens, if you don't know his voice, ride towards him and see who he is before you hark hounds to him. Upon principal, it is unwise to hark hounds to the cry of a first season hound. Upon windy and bad hearing days, keep close to your pack, and use your voice a good deal to keep your hounds pretty well together, for it is an easy thing upon a windy day for part of the pack to steal away upon a line without either you or the main body of hounds being aware of it.

When a fox is afoot, cheer your hounds forward to the leaders. Hounds scattered here, there, and everywhere, running one fox, present a sloppy picture. Cheer and encourage them to get together upon the line, and don't let anybody tell you nay. You can help your hounds much in this fashion, particularly in a hilly country when sometimes hounds on the other slope can't hear each other very well. Don't be afraid to use your voice upon such occasions, for through its proper use you aid the pack in a great way.

Down upon "Lick Creek," the expression upon the occasion of a bad loss is, "He's thowed 'em." The term "bad loss" means a real difficulty, of course. This happens chiefly when scenting is poor. It's a rare thing for a good pack to completely lose a running fox, — if scent is right. But if the scenting is mediocre, the worst is to be expected. I have seen hounds driving a fox across open country suddenly throw up their heads in pasture and never regain the line. But this rare sort of thing borders upon magic, and its explanation is difficult.

Old negroes were convinced that foxhounds would run a ghost, and things happen which lend substance to the belief. Certainly there is more of the mysterious in this game than seems reasonable in a world grown dependent upon factual data. "Smart as a fox," is no idle phrase. At least, no other animal, no deer, wolf, bobcat nor lion displays such cunning. Because of the clever stratagems which a fox employs to throw hounds off, as well as because of his beauty, gameness, and speed, foxhunters really love the animals they chase. And when upon some rare occasion a straight running fox is killed, pride in the feat is always tinged with sorrow. I never knew an American foxhunter that really wanted to kill a game fox. "He will run another day," is the always repeated expression. But all feel annoyed when beaten by wile and cunning, and every huntsman seems more frustrated upon these occasions than if he had missed his dinner. However, no hunter wants to see any unfair advantage taken of a fox. The rules of the sport are unwritten but as well established as those brought down from Sinai. At the first Washington Court House Ohio National Hunt years ago, a photographer hid in a ditch and got a wonderful closeup of a hard driven fox. But his act turned the fox back into the hounds, and the infuriated riders nearly mobbed the cameraman.

What is likely to cause hounds to lose the line? Ordinarily, a team ploughing, men at work, an automobile, a cur dog, sheep, or cattle, or fertilized land. Cattle bother hounds more than sheep do. However, I once saw a fox use a flock of sheep to mask his line in a perfect fashion. Hounds were driving an old and familiar fox up "Swinney Hollow," a valley near Hillsboro. He had perhaps a quarter of a mile lead but was tired when he came into a field near a flock of about fifty ewes. They huddled as he approached. He then gave a leap and landed well into the huddle upon a sheep's back. For several minutes he maintained the jockey role, first upon one and then upon another, until their frantic rush brought them near the woodland which bordered the side of the field. Then he dismounted, and I am sure bid them adieu in the Shavian manner. The hounds burst into the field a minute later with a roar of a cry, but when they came to the place where our hero had mounted his steeds and ridden away, they were like a bunch of ants whose house has been wrecked, and ran backwards and forwards for five minutes, until a smart bitch called "Reno" tried forward into the wood and found where the old musketeer had made his exit. And his brilliant exploit saved him, for he reached his hole and lived to run many another day.

When hounds check, be sure that you remember the place where they ceased to cry. The kind of a place it is, and the scent as well, affect your decision upon this matter. If it has been good scenting and hounds throw up their heads in a meadow, the fox made a sharp turn and hounds overran the line. If upon a good scenting day the loss is upon plough, press them on in the direction he was last going, in hopes of hitting it off ahead upon the grass. If the scent is spotty, take it easy at the losses and let the hounds circle until they recover the line, or until you are sure that they aren't going to do so within a reasonable time. Always remember in hunting a fox that he is going on. He isn't waiting around to let you puzzle out a loss. He is going on down to the store, or wherever the foxes loaf, and tell "the boys" how you fumble around. Of course, you can bore a fox to death by keeping hounds forever yodeling upon his line, but, if you want to really run one, you mustn't linger at every tobacco patch. On the contrary you must take chances when necessary. Fox hunting is a sport, a bold free one, and as ill suited for slow training as opossum hunting is for drive and speed.

When hounds run a hot line and suddenly throw up their heads, and are at loss, it is a ten to one bet that they have over-run. And if there is a loss involved, it is a certainty. As long as the faintest evanescent hint lingers of scent ahead, a good hound will try on. But to confess to himself that he over-ran the line is bitter medicine to take and, rightly enough, he generally tries back only after he has failed upon the other three chances. The sharp double back is one of a fox's best stratagems, and when hard pressed he makes full use of it. One time when we were running a fox hard through the hills just east of the Boston schoolhouse, (which is still an all rail country), he doubled back through the eight or ten horsemen as indifferently as though they were so many stalks of corn. And the audacious exploit was well rewarded, for the air was drenched with the scent of steaming horses and men, not to mention eau de cologne, and hounds simply couldn't distinguish Red's scent among such highly competitive odors, and, had they not been cheered onto the line, would have been long delayed.

If your fox runs a road, look for hounds to overrun when he turns off of it. It happens frequently enough to be axiomatic that hounds will drive so hard down a road that they will miss his turn. The fox rarely inclines off a road, but turns sharply at right angles. He almost always leaves the road upon the side opposite from his entry. When you bring hounds back, encourage them to try over the fence upon that side. When a hunted fox approaches a road, he won't often cross if there is any movement upon it. Instead, he will swing off at right angles. If you see a rider, a wagon, or a car far ahead, you can calculate that the fox will swing in the opposite direction to the one they are traveling. He has no thought of jogging along in the sight of any driver. So you can count that movement upon the road will "turn the fox." If the travelers have already passed, however, he may turn in that direction.

Remember that a fox doesn't just aimlessly run, like a mule in a pasture trying to escape boredom, but upon the contrary knows all the time where he is going. If headed, he will detour, but will try to continue his route. Upon his "home grounds" he will circle and try to return to the vicinity of his own sanctuary, — just in case he may need it. He will run almost the same route time after time, unless pressed. If hounds get close upon him, he will fail to make a turn sometimes, and be forced to pursue a less familiar route. If driven hard enough, he will go anywhere, even through a crowd of people. I don't think that he is so much afraid of people as that he dislikes the smell of soap. He certainly will run by a negro with little apparent concern.

Foxes don't hesitate to come around upon the same circle several times. This is the reason foot people manage to see so much of a chase. Perched upon a hill or a gatepost, or mounted on "Shank's pony," many see and hear more of a run than do the hardest riders. Only when hounds "take him out of the country" are they disappointed.

Sometimes a fox will run the top of a stone fence. If you suspect this, turn hounds along it until they come to the place where he got down. The sharp double back is another cause of checks. A fast, hard driving pack will generally swing wide ahead at a loss and only the seasoned veteran hastens back to make sure about a double. After your hounds have tried ahead, turn back and encourage them to consider the possibility of this trick, but "let them work the ground now with care."

Again a fox will run up to a hole and double right back upon his line. This frequently creates the conviction that he has gone in, although old hounds are not often long delayed by the wile. Thin bare ground causes trouble at times. If you lose in such a place, see that hounds don't delay there long, but encourage them to try in the most likely direction ahead. When hounds are checked among cattle, the same advice holds, they should try on beyond the area where the ground is foiled. If they try to work the line through, you will, I promise, be too long delayed.

I wish I had made notes on each day of the past few years of the conditions surrounding every check. Perhaps with such evidence, one might be able to offer some sound advice. But I only recall one in a thousand, and shall go out tomorrow and become again bewildered by what seems a new play. Fortunately, the hounds have better memories.

If you are new at hunting, set out to learn the habits of the foxes. When do they venture abroad, where do they go and why? What do they eat? How do they manage the whole business of taking a living from this old world? You can't absorb much of this information from a book. This is father to son, word of mouth learning that passes down through the ages, enriched by the observation of each generation, and a little of it is lost each time a grey bearded hunter goes to join his fathers in the churchyard.

100 "GONE AWAY!"

A lone hound was reaching for his brush.

And then you must learn how foxes act when they are hunted. Here, there is first a general field of knowledge, for foxes, like angels, have, I am told, some habits common to the genus. But each fox also has some special wiles of his own. He runs certain routes, is apt to use an especial trick or two upon occasions, and can best be driven from his cover in a particular way. These things you should know.

Some foxes gain great fame by their speed and cunning, and live to a ripe old age, honored like a great racehorse or an athlete. Their victories over local hounds are heralded about, and man comes then from far counties to pit famous hounds against them. The greatest of these "races" are part of the folklore of communities for generations. A quarter of a century ago near Bowling Green, Kentucky, there was a fox called "The Smallhouse Fox," so named because he lived in a thicket hard by the "Smallhouse Pike." I ran him a couple of years, and finally invited the county's best to meet him. Bob Rodes, General Seibert, the Doty Brothers and Joe Kirby came bringing their hounds. The harvest moon looked down upon sixty good hounds that night, and when they were cast, the fox circled time and again, in a forty acre cornfield, as was his custom. He always ran like a grey at first, short circles and a lot of twisting and dodging. Upon bad scenting days, these tactics frequently proved to be "sufficient to throw hounds" off.

"Must be a Grey!" someone snorted.

Bob Rodes asked me pointedly if I knew for sure that he was a "Red." That question answered itself shortly afterwards. For a half hour he ran those short circles, and the indignation of my friends waxed high. Then suddenly, like an arrow from a bow, he shot out of the cornstalks across the open wheatfields, and never turned for seven miles. When he came back, he had twenty-one hounds with him. An hour later he had twelve. Then, he set out for Simpson County, fifteen miles west. Just before sunup, we heard far in the distance a lone hound coming back, giving his coarse chop mouth with the regularity of a locomotive on a grade. I was sure that it was my hound, "Lead," until someone observed that dejected adventurer lying behind me with his feet to the fire. Each in turn sincerely identified the approaching hound as his own, but only the Doty boys were right. When the fox went by us in the moonlight, a lone hound was reaching for his brush, — Doty's "Ole Bob." Fifty-nine hounds were strewn across that countryside, many I fear with hot feet in the air; some still trying, — but far behind. All had enough! It is well to meet one of these great foxes occasionally, so that you may really find out what kind of hounds you have.

If your fox lives in a big wood, take all your pack with you. The larger the wood, the more good hounds it takes to push him into the open. His tactics here will generally be to circle and circle until his "track" is crossed and recrossed and hounds are strung out all over the place. Here you must try to keep in touch with your lead hounds, and, with liberal use of your voice, keep harking hounds to them. Try not to let the top hounds get away without the pack. It takes lots of attention and hard riding to do this. If the horn is ever justified after a fox is afoot, it is in these big woods. Even then, you must be chary of its use. Squeal it to get your hounds forward when first they hit him off, and, for the same reason upon recovery after bad losses, when the pack is scattered. But only use the horn when you feel it must carry farther than your voice. A horn loses its usefulness if frequently employed. Hunting a pack in a large woodland has one aim, to drive the fox into the open. To do this, hounds must push him hard. This means that you must be on the alert and unsparing of your horse and of yourself. Once the fox is up and running, noise at times has value, for only by timely and generous use of your voice will you be able to hold your pack together. Most large wooded areas are also hilly and rough. In these, hounds get out of touch with each other. It is then easy for a few hounds to get away with the line unheard by their fellows. Your job is to let them all know what is going on. As you top a rise, following either trailing or running hounds, tap your horn or cheer your hounds so that those behind may locate you. For if left behind in a valley, they may hear nothing of the cry and continue to hunt oblivious to the chase ahead.

When running along a small stream, the fox will frequently slip away from it in great or lesser arcs, only to return further along to the valley. Even if pushed, he may wait for his especial spot to leave the valley. Should you attempt to follow him each time, you lose distance toiling up hills, around cliffs, etc., when, had you stayed in the vale, you would have been in closer touch with your hounds. So you must know this fox's run, that you may leave only at the right place and reach the top of the tableland hard after him. Here again you must use horn or voice liberally, for it may be the last chance scattered hounds behind you in the valley will have of hearing cry ahead.

When the fox is crossing big open country, a knowledge of his route will enable you to assist stragglers. Perhaps he will cross a wired-up farm where you cannot follow. Make haste now to "cut" and get on to his next "crossing." Take with you what hounds have been thrown out, and go in haste, for you may succeed in putting them on the line close behind the pack. As the pack passes, cheer vigorously, both for the pack and for the help it will afford hounds further back. As the pack passes you must press after it in order to encourage it in victory, or to rally it at a loss. In an open country, many checks offer solution via your own eyes. You must learn how to look ahead for the fox. His peculiarly individual movements will arrest your eye, as does the swoop of crows, the gallop of colts in a pasture, the scurry of a flock, or any other evidence of the passing fugitive. And ahead, the kaleidoscopic scene should imprint itself upon your brain: the wagon coming down the lane, the ploughman in the field, the cattle in the pasture, for any of these things may cause difficulties. Very few men ever try to help a pack of hounds in any way. That is quite fortunate, for few can be of much help. What we are talking about now is not night hunting, and not Field Trials, but the pursuit of the fox by a *pack,* and the object of this pursuit is to run the fox as hard, and as swiftly as possible. So when you see the hunted fox cross out of George Herbert's wood and head for "Maple Grove," have pity upon your canine pals who still are puzzling out his line where he was headed in the opposite direction. *You* may not have a nose, but you have a voice. Why sit there and let your hounds toil across a rocky half mile when a cheer will set them that much closer to their fox? It seems that many of us lose sight of the fact that the competition is between the pack and the fox, and view the chase as a match between individual hounds. That is why you hear men speak proudly of the duration of a chase.

"We ran him for four hours," or "he ran until sunup," are common expressions of pride among night hunters. But few foxes should elect to stay above ground in front of a well balanced pack, in a country free of woven wire fences, for any such period of time.

"Don't do as I do, do as I say," is the defense of every preacher with a straying eye or a dry throat. And I must plead guilty to a like charge, for I find it hard these days to keep my pack disciplined and unified. Tennessee is a wooded hilly country for the most part, and that type of country is more conductive to the development of Andrew Jacksons and Cordell Hulls than to disciplined masses. The same thing is true of hounds. From "Tennessee Lead" down to last year's National Champion, "Kentucky Buzzard," the area has produced many great individual hounds, but perhaps few great packs. A great pack is a group of really good hounds of like characteristics trained to hunt as a unit. To train them to so hunt requires first, daily exercise together. And then it demands a lot of hunting in an open country of small woodlands, — and a few foxes. In such a country a hound must get away with the pack if he is to have any sport, whereas in a hilly country, full of foxes, he cheerfully goes off, maybe with one of his friends, and runs a fox on his own. Again, in an open country, any difference in speed and endurance between pack members becomes quickly apparent, for a straight running fox in such a country soon reduces everything to a common denominator, and the hound that can't run with the pack, or that has a shadow of yellow upon his shield, "stands out," as Dick Peak used to say, "like an outhouse in a fog at Newtonville."

The problems that come up in the field to a man hunting foxhounds are rarely twice the same. I don't think that Br'er Fox is in league with the Devil, but evidently some time back they must have been upon friendly terms. Somewhere the head of the fox family picked up a lot of devilish tricks that continue to confuse both hound and man.

Huntsmen are largely divided into two classes, those that attempt to help their hounds too much, and those that help them too little, or not at all. The latter are in the great majority in the South. The night hunter measures his "races" by hours, the longer the better. But the pack hunter is expected home for dinner and has promised to help the children with their algebra problems, or made some other equally vague commitment, so he must get on with the chase. An illustration or two of his field problems may be of some value.

For example:

The fox is up and hounds have been driving him hard across a rather open country for ten minutes. You are galloping up with them and can see every individual hound. Just ahead, bordering the meadow hounds are in, is a little rivulet fringed by low brush. When hounds strike it, they swing sharp left and the cry dies out in a hundred yards. About half the pack, including some top hounds, press on to the left across another meadow, casting wide, and fast. These are quite obviously going to hunt a long way in that direction. The remainder double back upstream towards you. There is a little uncertain cry and then silence. A number of good hounds cast back and far to the right in wide circles.

Straight ahead and down wind is a half mile of sticky plough and beyond it some trees. Two young hounds are hunting ahead on this in a doubting fashion, but have not opened once nor even whimpered. The sun is getting hotter every minute and you know that scent is failing fast. What should you do? If the fox had turned right in the meadow, or doubled back into the wind, the hounds would have picked up his line, and the hounds that swung left have gone too far without cry. Should you wait until some wide casting hound circles beyond the plough? One doubtless will before long, but if he hits it there he will be a half mile ahead of a badly scattered pack when he does. Far to the right near there is a ploughman yelling. Does he see the fox? Just before the loss, you confided to a distinguished visitor that this was probably the best pack in the South! What is the answer?

Send someone to the left to turn those hounds to you. Sound your horn and gallop down wind straight across the plough towards the fringe of trees. Stop before you get into them and let the hounds spread. There's a dirt road between the plough and the strip of woodland ahead. Now you recall seeing a horse and buggy passing on it to the right a few minutes previously. Not a hound has whimpered, — but some of your friends have. The minutes pass. What shall you do now? Just then, far to the right, you catch sight of "Reno" at the side of the road, head down and stern flying. She whimpers twice. Good bitch! She is going to save you yet. She cries it!

"Hark to Reno!" bursts from your throat. Hounds come tumbling back out of the wood, they honor her, and away you go again on the Glory Road. You may not be of much assistance with the algebra that night, but reflection over the day's work assures you that your mathematical weakness does not eminate from a lack of brains.

Or again; it is a poor scenting day. It is getting late. Hounds have been trailing a "walking fox" for an hour. They seem unable to get ahead with it. The sky is overcast and the air smells like rain. You are twelve miles from home and ahead of you lies a rough, wild country of great hills and woodlands. If you get into it you will be until a late hour gathering hounds. Your wife has just reminded you that an old friend is coming to dinner. Just then, far ahead, you hear "Mischief's" voice, clear and positive, "Its hot as a firecracker," he says. And you know he's never wrong, and hates a cold line like a horse does elephants. Not a hound has heard it. You look back and note that your Field waits with patient confidence, but have either not heard the cry or have attached no significance to it.

What do you do?

Well just then your friend, Eugene Harris, who rides like a centaur, never tires, and knows all there is to know about every hound in the Pack, calls to you, "Mischief has the line, hot — straight ahead." Your problem is solved. You won't get home until midnight.

Another problem: The sun shone warm all day yesterday. Today the air is crisp and cold. The Inglehame fox came tumbling out of his bed and was off like a bullet immediately the first hound spoke. The pack is away on the instant. You could "cover them all with a blanket." The fox turns South across a sod country with some stone walls and rail mixed in with the omnipresent wire. You give the "gone away" and settle down to ride. Everything pleases everybody. The bold and the fair soar over the first wall like swallows at eventide. Suddenly, in the middle of a close cropped pasture, the cry stops. Hounds frantically cast themselves in widening circles, but no music results. Five minutes pass. The fox has pulled the Indian rope trick and vanished into thin air. What should you do? Fifty yards behind you is the wall you leaped to get into the pasture. Hounds circled back that far at once and returned. You call the near hounds to you and go back over the wall. They hunt along that side of it each way without success. To your left, as you first approached, the country is open, to the right a half mile away is a small thickly covered hill. You hunt toward it. Suddenly, "Startle" leaps to the top of the wall and cries the line. Then you raise the echoes to hark the pack to her, — and are away again.

What did the fox do that caused the check? Perhaps he never crossed the wall at all but leaped upon it and turned right. Even the best pack, when scent is dull and the pace is swift will overrun the line at times. Or maybe the fox was turned, doubled quickly back upon his own line and topped the wall. Would it not have been as wise to have sat still and waited until some of your hounds had circled into the wooded hill? Probably so. But you certainly helped to shorten the time lost and got on better terms with your fox.

Foxhunting is not a science, its an art. If its vagaries could be calculated the fun would be gone. Each time you take hounds to the field, something new turns up. The last chase is never like the preceding one. You may hunt wild foxes in a natural country for fifty years and upon the last hunt, as upon the first one, the wiley Red Ranger may leave you bemuddled.

Now and again upon poor scenting days hounds are unable to get their fox running. They don't lose the line, nor do they seem to get on with it. The fox is just toddling on ahead in no great hurry, but hounds can't press him. Foxes that act this way are referred to as "walking foxes," and that is the gait they *seem* to travel. We followed one once long ago from Pine Wood Road through Mitchems Forest six miles to a point way down upon "South Harper," and never had a loss nor hounds in a gallop. My advice upon this sort of a situation has no great value. Certainly you should crowd your hounds as much as possible. Better hounds is the real answer. The aggressive, driving hound dislikes such a line more than you do, and will press it time after time to get forward. Once he gets close to the fox, that sardonic gentleman will get on his way. If you have at present no such hounds and encounter a strolling devil of a fox, ride close to your lead hounds, keep them stirred up, and get someone ahead to chance a view. If he succeeds, let him "halloa" as stoutly as he can.

In the great majority of cases, anything you do to help a pack of hounds is wrong. And if you don't let them try on their own, until they give it up or scatter too far, you will make a mistake. However, now and then you can be helpful. And perhaps most frequently by keeping two or three of your real "fox finders" under close observation and then getting the pack quickly to them when they hit it off. It is not always recognized how much depends upon the sense of one or two of the elders in a pack. Experience is as valuable as nose, drive or speed, and that trinity of virtues will not suffice to press a fox, unless coupled with some match for his cunning.

In a "thick" country, that is one full of trees or brush where a fox may do much of his running in cover, it is not always immediately discernible from the cry which way the gentleman is headed, or, in the vernacular, which hound has "the top of it." For example, after a bad loss, when hounds are widely scattered, several may pick up separated segments of a circle at the same time, and you may have good hounds crying an *uncovered* line in opposite, or variable, directions. If hills or cedar brakes separate them, two sections of a pack may not even hear each other. Unless you lend some assistance, this means that your pack will be badly strung out before the "bottom" hounds get up to the covered track. Of course, if they are good hounds, they will no longer cry the line then, but will race forward to the cry ahead.

In an open country, if you are so fortunate as to hunt one, this sort of thing is of rarer occurrence. For one thing, the fox is apt to have been viewed, or his run is easier to determine. In an open grass country, such as the beautiful part of the "Iroquis" country laying back from the Kentucky river, the problem is, I daresay, rather to maintain a balanced pack, than one with fast hounds in it. Wide casting hounds might string a pack out badly, even though the checks were short. And a fox can run far better with a slow pack composed of hounds that run and cast alike, than with a faster pack not well matched. Of course, we all dream of a fast, wide casting pack, somewhat uniform in speed. My experience is that it takes years to build one (if you have to find out all the secrets yourself) and by that time you are about ready for a slow pack. The old saying that one "can't buy experience with the other fellow's money," appears to be sound. And few of us like advice about horses or hounds. When we are young, we can't take advice because we have a different set of values. A father tells a son that, "there is nothing to that girl but a pretty figure, blonde hair, and a pair of big blue eyes." These, of course, are the only qualities the boy is looking for. And so it is with foxhunting. The chap under thirty likes his fences high, and pace swift. It is not until he has been hunting a long time that he begins to seek for "honor, faith and a sure intent." So there are few good foxhunters without a sprinkle of salt at the temples. And, after some mistaken crosses have used up years, there is not overmuch time to build a really top pack. Really, it's a three generation job.

Frequently in hill country, and more frequently during the mating season, the pack is apt to split and to run two foxes. This situation is sometimes accidental, but often, I am sure, a matter of arrangement by foxes. I have seen them do great entangling figure eights, with the lines crossing and recrossing in opposite directions. A good honest hound, that never goes near a dram shop, can come out of one of these mazes as confused as a sailor after three hours in the old French Quarter in New Orleans.

One time in the "Holly Tree Gap Hills," two foxes tangled fourteen couple of good hounds into such knots that at one stage of the affair two groups of hounds met head on in a hillside field. I was sitting upon my horse high above and saw the two foxes meet. They chatted doubtless about previous romances, the rabbit crop, and such things, until the scream of approaching hounds warned them to be on their way. Then one trotted forward and doubled back and the other turned right toward the hounds approaching him. Although I sat there looking at the maneuver, I couldn't follow the trick. But a minute later hounds were running in every direction, bawling and disputing like lawyers in a squire's court. When contretemps of the sort occur, what should the men hunting hounds do? In this case, we marked the course of the fox that went in a direction that might carry him out of the hills, and galloping after him drew, by aid of voice and horn, as many hounds with us as we could. The fox that headed away from the hills proved to be the dog fox out from home upon a visit, and we had a good run with the bulk of the pack.

Foxes will also play the game of relay. One will tire and will persuade a friend to take his place. This, of course, doubtless occurs more frequently by accident than by design, but it may be a planned maneuver as well. However, in any country most of us will hunt, there is not much to be done about this trick. In a country where the fox may be readily viewed, opportunity to distinguish between the hunted fox and the fresh one occur. Of course, when you view a fox that is dragging his feet, is "down by the stern," and has his tongue out, it is natural to assume that he is the hunted fox. But in much of the country where some of us must hunt, the woods are so thick, and the weeds so high, that it would be difficult to distinguish a difference of appearance between an ox and an elephant, to say nothing of foxes.

A fox crossing a field leaves a track of scent oil.

CHAPTER XI

SCENT

No one ever really understood scent until 1933 when Mr. H. M. Budgett published his book, "HUNTING BY SCENT." And without study of this book, a real understanding of the subject is a practical impossibility. It is one of the most useful of all books concerned with Hunting. Most of the comments upon scent which follow are based upon the principles Mr. Budgett developed.

A fox crossing a field leaves a track of scent oil. The hound doesn't smell these particles of oil but smells the air that has come into contact with them. Hot air rises. Therefore, scent will be best when the temperature of the ground is warmer than the air. This is why the fox hunts at night, as this condition then generally exists. When the sun starts down, the air cools much more rapidly than the earth. In the later afternoon, scent most frequently starts to improve. A few days of warm weather followed by a sudden cold spell brings the right condition. There is seldom good scent during bright sunshine, unless a cool breeze is blowing. If snow falls before a frost, it insulates and keeps warm the ground, so scent may then be good.

If snow falls after a hard frost, it keeps the ground cold and scent may be bad for a long time. A sudden fall in temperature brings good scent. A sudden rise means bad scent. If the days have been warm and it starts to turn cool, go hunting. But if there has been a spell of cold weather, and it turns warm, leave the hounds in the kennel.

If your good hounds are listless and disinterested, scent is bad. Some hounds can't read, but all of them can tell you whether it will be a good or a bad day to hunt. When the ground is warmer than the air, hounds are full of zest. Trotting down the lane upon such a day, they get a news record of their world as complete for them as is your morning newspaper for you. But when they stand around and look at you, like a Midshipman at a movie star, the ground is colder than the air and you had better ride down to the crossroads store and hitch your horse, for the hunting will be poor that morning.

Upon some days scent may be good in the open but bad in the woods. Probably this happens when the sun has been out the day before and warmed the open ground but wasn't out long enough to warm the ground in the woods where there was insulation by a carpet of leaves and shade by the trees. When the sun rather suddenly gets hot while you are hunting, notice how much better scent is in the woods than in the open. This is because the shaded woodland air warms more slowly.

To test Mr. Budgett's theory requires two thermometers. One you put in the ground far enough to cover up the mercury bulb, the other is hung a couple of feet above it. When the lower one reads 5° higher than the upper one, scent will be excellent. When they both read the same, scent will be fair, but when the bottom thermometer is colder than the top one, scent will be bad.

Of course, one temperature reading won't insure the hunting all day, but it is a fairly certain indicator of what you may expect for the next few hours. The temperature of the ground changes quite slowly, rarely as much as 5° in a normal day, but the air may change 25°, or more, any day. When the temperatures of the ground and of the air are the same, reasonable scenting conditions prevail. When the ground is 3° warmer, hounds can drive a fox, and when it is 4° and upwards, they can make the Red Rover abandon romance and seek safety. Generally, during the Fall, scent starts to improve around four o'clock (sun time). Later on, the improvement begins as early as three o'clock. From then on, the air is cooling faster than the earth. When I was a boy, I was supposed to turn homeward at dusk, and it was just then that the cry of the pack always sounded as though they were going to catch him. From sunset to shortly after sunrise, the scent is normally good. Most of the time when you start hunting in the morning, scent is going to steadily grow weaker as the sun gets higher. Normally from eleven until two-thirty conditions are at their worst.

In the wintertime, the air generally begins to cool between three and four o'clock in the afternoon. The "three o'clock fox" is proverbial for so many have been started at that time of the day. If you hunt at daybreak, the favorable temperature relationship still holds, but will worsen each hour.

If you hunt all day, it is wise to give hounds and horses a rest for a couple or three hours during the bad scenting time in the middle of the day. If you keep good hounds, it is a mistake to push them upon these bad scenting days. If you have regular afternoon fixtures and have to go upon certain days, take your hounds to a far distant cover and try to arrive there as late as possible. No good hound, if he feels well, needs to be encouraged to hunt, we have all seen them hunt with terrible wounds, broken bones and other sorts of handicaps. But if scenting conditions are bad, the hound must wonder about us. After all, he thinks that your nose is just like his, and that you know everything, — or should anyhow.

There is usually good scent in fog of course, because fogs are brought about by moisture rising from warm ground into cooler air. Scent holds better upon sod then any place else. And, conversely, worse upon plough. When, however, there has been a quick, upward movement in temperature, plough warms faster, and, for a short period, will carry better scent. When plough "picks up," is sticky and gathers upon a foxes' foot as he goes over it, there is practically no scent. Scent isn't good when the ground is covered with hoarfrost. Sunshine damages scent. However, if a cool breeze is blowing at the same time, scent will carry well. After a long cold spell, followed suddenly by a warm one, hunt in the woods, — if you must hunt. Scent is generally better on moist than on dry ground. The scent oil spreads over a wider surface of moist ground. But if temperature relationships are right, hounds can drive a fox even though the ground is dusty.

Hounds can't really run fast upon a line over thirty minutes old. They know in advance when scent is good or bad. If it is good, they sniff at everything. If bad, they don't bother. Watch them when they come out of the kennel. If scent is good, they are full of energy and difficult to restrain. If it is bad, they stand around like a hill farmer at a barbecue, wondering what to do next.

A sudden fall in temperature brings good scenting conditions. A sudden rise brings bad ones. Foxhunting is really a sport designed by the gods to make you happy upon a bad day. If the weather starts to "fair up" there is plenty to do upon the land for everybody. But if the air starts to chill and the day grow a little uncomfortable, the world is yours . . . then is the time to take your horn off the mantel and to open the kennel door.

Automobile exhausts, beech and oak leaves (particularly in the fall), burned-over or fertilized ground, wild onions, mustard, mint (and many other plants), damage the scent of the fox. Water does not destroy scent, but scatters it. When the streams and ponds are "smoking," scent is good. An approaching storm ruins scent. But when the rain commences to patter, scenting conditions rapidly improve. All these facts about scent are true most of the time but, "once in a blue moon," when conditions appear to be wrong, hounds will get up a fox and run him hard. That, I suppose is like the "lagnappe" the storekeeper in New Orleans gives you when you make a purchase.

There are two natural laws with which every fox hunter should be thoroughly acquainted. The first and most important is Feland's Law:

"If you drink too much whiskey, you will get drunk." There is no necessity of further experiment to test the validity of that law. The second law is also worth remembering and equally true, if the ground is colder than the air, scent is bad.

HOUND WAYS

Each of your hounds has as much individuality as the riders who follow them. To hunt hounds, you must know these individual characteristics as a schoolboy knows his A. B. C.'s. Suppose we illustrate the temper, disposition and hunting ways of a few hounds.

Take "Mischief" for example. He is a four season dog hound, will never cry anything but a fox under any circumstances. Knowing this, you look always to him, or to one like him, for confirmation of a doubtful line. And what a help that is! But he can be very annoying. He won't hunt at all upon a bad scenting day, nor in a country that he believes to be bare of foxes. Like a man, he gets bored and wants to go home. When he is hunting, he pays no attention to the movement of other hounds, but when cast, makes his way directly to where he thinks a fox lies. He harks only to the cry of a few contemporaries in whom he has confidence, and regards everybody else, including you, as a tyro at the game. How do you work with such a hound? Well, you try to always have him in the corner of your eye, or to keep one ear cocked for his voice. If you can't, you get your Whip or some dependable friend to keep contact with him, and you hark hounds to him without hesitation when he cries a line.

Then, there's "Reno." She's a ball of fire in the field, hunts at top speed and has the best nose in the pack. At a check, you never lose contact with her. She has an unusually high pitched voice. When she cries at a loss, you hark hounds to her at once. But when she is *first* trying to find a fox, you don't. She's not quite steady then and rabbit may tempt her. You always wait for a "trusty" to honor her cry upon these ocasions.

When "Dennis" cries, the fox is up. He is the hound you pivot on, he does everything as it should be done. At the cast, he changes general direction with your horse, hunts only where a fox might be, but misses nothing. At a loss, he casts himself in concentric circles at a gallop. And when his deep voice sounds, you don't need to hark the others to him, — they rush towards him with a confidence born of experience.

Here's "Lead," a five season hound, true, and with a stellar nose and voice. But this season you suspect is his last. The speed of the young ones may have made him jealous. He is beginning to stay over-long at a check, to turn back at little losses. Watch him, for he may start to dwell a bit one of these days.

Now comes "Gratitude," a fast, hard driving, top running bitch. But she's like her sister "Gene," and both, like their mother, — would rather run than hunt. And, too, she never seems to lose interest in sheep or anything that moves. Watch her. Then there is "Beauty," faultless and true. But don't expect her to find the fox. Pay no attention to her at the cast. She has her nose in every clump of grass, and the fox is found long before she reaches his bed. But at a check, listen for her. That careful, patient way of hers frequently unravels the knot. "Startle" is like her, but with a touch of genius in her nose. She won't take a chance and cast far ahead, but she will solve the puzzle of a loss so many times that you must always be listening for her cry. Her sister, "Stainless," also has a grand nose, is faultless and with a touch of speed that carries her further afield at a check. What about the three (first season) Graces, "Dolly," "Sinful," and "Stealth." They are very fast hounds you are sure. But be chary with your confidence. "Dolly" has a way of looking at sheep as she passes them. She teems with energy, she may become a great hound. She might get into trouble. Keep your eye on her. "Sinful" had an amour that seems to have steadied her down. She seems outstanding, but you must reserve judgment until you have hunted her more. "Stealth" is a great hound. Although this is her first season, she is made. When she crys, its a fox. How she drives on the line, and turns with it, though at top speed! Treat her like a lady, trust her, — she merits it.

"Plato" runs hard when a fox is up, behaves perfectly on the road and is very responsive to horn and voice, but "Plato" is developing a vice. When younger he was over fond of rabbits, but received so much of the lash when he cried them that he is silent about it now unless you are a good distance from him. He practically never finds a fox nor straightens out a loss, but just gallops behind a driving pack. He is nearly what dairymen call a "boarder" and next season, when the new entry comes on, is going to be drafted.

"Van Dyke" is in his second season and is a hard driving, slashing sort of a hound but he is not steady about riot, and the line of a cur dog will lead him astray. Perhaps a few good thrashings will cure this bold buccaneer, but, if they don't, you must part with him before he has led the younger hounds into bad habits. "Moonshine" is a problem, terribly fast and incurably jealous. She always tries to steal the line and gets further and further ahead before she opens. She will make some night hunter happy, but shouldn't stay in the pack. "General" is a fine looking big hound, but the truth is that "he can't take it." When the pace gets too hot for him, he will at times drop back and continue to open on the covered track. Then at a bad loss, the young hounds hear his great authoritative voice and go back to see about it. The place for him is in a drag pack at an army post. "Michael" has been a wonderful hound with a voice so deep and sonorous that it wakes the echoes. But the old boy has a touch of arthritis. At a cast, if he doesn't find the fox himself, he ignores any other cry and deliberately goes off in search of his own fox. He knows that he can't dance to the tune the others sing, so he tries to conduct a sideshow of his own. Farewell, Old Man, go up on the mountain and teach some small boy to be a foxhunter. So it goes. When the pack trots down the road, they look as much alike as the Rockette Ballet at Radio City, but alas, they are not. Babblers, skirters and cheats are hidden under as good coats as honest, bold and true gentlemen wear. And to have a real pack, you must be done with these, for "bad companions corrupt good manners."

Shame them for their misbehaviour.

CHAPTER XII

THE WHIPPER-IN ALIAS THE WHIP

If this position had carried the designation of "Assistant Huntsman," much damage would have been averted, for many a man upon receiving the accolade of "Whip" has assumed that handiness with the thong was the chief qualification for the job. And what a lot of ruinous popping and cracking has been done! A foxhound is particularly frightened by noise, and a few pops of the whip as he comes out of the kennel door may make him timid for the ensuing year. Good advice to a Whipper-in would be not to crack his whip, except when a hound actually disobeys basic laws. These forbid running sheep, cur dogs, rabbits, or anything else but a fox. They also prescribe the killing of chickens, baying livestock, or people. An obstinate refusal to obey orders should perhaps be included in this category. Generally speaking, a quiet nip with a whip has a better corrective value than when preceded by a high explosive popping. Loud sounds jars the nerves of hounds, but pain doesn't, it is a corrective they use themselves, and well understand. There are now and then hounds that require a lot of correction whilst others shrink and cringe at the first indication of roughness in a voice. A good man with hounds should understand these peculiarities and temper his tone to suit the individual. For what else should a hound be whipped? There is little else. Or shall we state it differently, there is little else when the whip should be used with sound effects, except perhaps a cut at a recalcitrant who insists upon carrying a long "departed" rabbit or an ancient fowl he finds at the roadside. The use of the whip upon a pack of hounds should be proportioned like "tabasco" sauce, of which a very little is helpful, but more spoils the dinner.

"Now," says our Whipper-in, "you have told me that I mustn't use my beautiful whip — what am I to do?" Well, my brave lad, you are to assist the man who hunts the hounds. You are the co-pilot. Suppose we start at the beginning. Your first duty is to know every hound, all his characteristics, his mama and papa, — and his voice. The latter is the most important of all. Suppose we are hunting a great wood cut through by cliffs and ravines. Far to the left you catch the cry of a lone hound. If its "Lowry" its a fox, but if its "Placable" it might be a "cotton-tail." Now it makes all the difference on earth whether you report to the Huntsman that Lowry has opened, or whether you can only say:

"A hound is speaking to our left." In the first case, the pack is harked to him with the certainty that a fox has been found; whereas in the latter case, ignorance of the voice and ways of the hound in question may either cause us to fail to support an honest hound, or to take the pack across a "Grand Canyon," — to discover a rabbit.

If you know all hounds by name, suppose we start at the kennel door as the pack comes out to go hunting. Here they come, heads and sterns up, and leap with joy around the Huntsman's horse. But one hound dashes gaily off as though to forever leave the pack. Should you gallop after him? You should not. Let him alone, for one hound rarely leaves a pack for long. But, as we go down the road, three youngsters make a dash for liberty. Turn them back if you can, for three constitutes conspiracy. But don't get too serious about it. Nine out of ten times they will rejoin the pack upon their own. The greatest mistakes "Whips" make are chasing hounds, and popping whips. Discipline is gained by long hours of exercise, not by sudden spurts of correction. Unless a hound is after sheep, or really in serious trouble, you waste time by a "stern chase." And when hounds are first out of kennels they are wild with joy. Like boys just out of school, or colts from a stable, they must play and gallop about a bit before they settle down to anything. If you would like to see hounds behave more sedately leaving kennels, take them out an hour before, and put them back when they have had a little frolic. They will then come out with a little more decorum. If your Huntsman wants the pack to walk out like young nuns from a convent, he must achieve the discipline by practice and not by correction.

We proceed to the meeting place. We arrive twenty minutes ahead of time. What do you do now? Well, you "ride herd" on the pack, as the cow-men say. You keep it together in quiet order, chiefly by use of your voice. And in this, too, your success is measured not by what you do or say at the moment, but by how much work you have put in upon the hounds in their training.

We start to the "cover" which may be a sedgegrass field overgrown with sassafras, or it may be a hundred acres of cedar forest carpeted by rocks. Now we have arrived and the Huntsman is about to cast hounds. Do you "post forward to the cover's end to tally-ho the fox?" You do nothing of the kind, unless you are also a Boswick and a magician. If he knows the run of this fox, the Huntsman tells you where he wants you to go, but, if he doesn't know, he probably says:

"Bill, you take the right flank. If we don't find him between here and Uncle Pig Stanfield's thicket, we will swing left to Ely's Woods." Then you ride along about an eighth of a mile away and keep your ears and eyes open. If hounds spread to your right and "hit it" there, you make sure that the Huntsman knows it. But you don't go galloping about to tell him. Remember this; hounds hardly ever burst a fox into a run. If you hear a sudden burst of cry after a cast, it is, as you know, ninety-nine times out of a hundred a "white tailed fox." Upon these lamentable occasions, your immediate duty needs no great explanation. You get to their heads and shame them for their misbehavior. If they do not promptly desist, you give them a taste of bitter tea. Ride right in among them, turning this way and that, and chide them as you would a negro caught sleeping in work time. In other words, the dash of young hounds after a rabbit is not anything to burst a blood vessel over. They quit these things whenever they learn that they are wrong.

You hear "Longstreet" open a half mile to your right. Now you slip over towards the Huntsman and advise him that the Oracle has spoken. He turns and harks hounds to the cry. You now swing back towards what was his left flank and get hounds on to him. You do this by first arresting their attention and then "hissing" them to cry. "Red Wings" for instance, is in a swag, nose to the ground, working through a briar thicket.

"Hark boy." "Hark!" you say in a voice just loud enough to catch his ear. His head comes up; if he can hear that far away cry, he needs no further admonition. If he can't hear it, you turn your horse's head and ride a little in that direction, hissing him forward meantime. If he is an old hound, he knows what you are trying to tell him and goes like blazes in the right direction. If he is a young one, he "follows the crowd" and learns in time what you mean when you use those words.

"Hark to 'em. Hark! Hark!" the huntsman will, of course cry aloud, but obviously two men doing this would confuse hounds. So yours is a sotto voice, a loud whispered combination of sounds, to get hounds heads up, and to appraise them of the fact that the fox has been found. Say what you will, but always use the same sounds upon these ocasions, so that the hounds understand you. Hissing, strained, lowtones are what you want, for you are now "whispering in the hound's ear" that Rome is burning. You must catch his attention, excite him, and move him in the right direction all at once. The hunting sounds men make vary as greatly as the cry of hounds. They are largely unintelligible because use has smoothed off the edges which made them words. The slurs and elusions that go to make a hunting language perfectly intelligible to you and to the hounds, are not conformable to any rules of syntax. Say what you will, provided your voice excites the right hounds without turning others back.

The huntsman is cheering the balance of the pack to "Longstreet" and most of them are galloping that way of their own accord. Hounds go quicker to any cry if cheered by their hunstman. His endorsement removes any doubt as to its validity. Now some "lead hounds" have hit the line ahead and the cry swells. The Huntsman is cheering on the tail hounds. Your work of getting hounds on is finished. Now what should you do? "Get to cry" is always the answer. But, if you know the run of this fox and are convinced that he will swing left, you push ahead that way. If you guessed correctly and no wire stops you, you may get to hounds now ahead of the Huntsman. Shall you proceed? Certainly, for he may never get there. Perhaps now his horse is down in wire. You go on with the hounds. When the Huntsman arrives, which we hope will be soon, put yourself at his disposal, either to go along protempts, to help him with the gates and wired up places or to get forward to the earth to turn the fox from "going in."

Suppose in the course of the run the Huntsman loses contact with the hounds? Your duty is to stay on with them and to take over his job until he shows up. This matter, however, must be handled with discretion, and as quietly as possible, for the pack may have split, and your efforts may be widening the breach. If you know the hounds, you soon know whether you have the main pack, or are off with a group of young revolutionists who are afte a fresh fox. If this is the case, break up the run when a check intervenes, get their heads up and gallop with them to the main pack.

When the run is over, your job is to collect hounds. There is no thrill to this and, if you are an amateur, you may want very much to chuck it and to get on home before night falls. If you must "catch the 6:15" upon hunting days, resign from the Whip's job. You can't handle a watch and a whip at the same time. It goes without saying that any Whip must be well mounted. And he must not be a cautious rider. A touch of the daredevil is a great asset. The fellow who will get to hounds when trouble threatens is worth his weight in gold. Time after time, I have seen my good friends John Sloan and Eugene Harris sail over "unjumpable places" and get to recalcitrant hounds when an instant's delay might have meant a witches' cauldron of trouble. This quality of boldness is the greatest one a Whip can have. Nothing is so valued by a hunting Master as the knowledge that he is supported by valor.

Eight miles from home.

CHAPTER XIII

HORSES

Horses occupy a place of undue importance in the minds of many people who foxhunt.

> "Poor Jack . . .
> Lived in his saddle, loved the Chase,
> the course,
> And always 'ere he mounted, kissed his
> horse."

This is as perhaps it should be. It certainly helps hunt subscriptions.

People will listen to advice at times about land, money, travel and other subjects. An occasional young lady will even listen to her mother about a beau, but no one ever takes advice about a horse. So this brief chapter is of less value than the ink that prints it. However, I cannot resist one comment upon the subject. The purpose of a hunting horse is to carry you to the hounds, and to keep you near them, with little fuss and with maximum security. The more tractable a horse is in the hunting field, the better suited he is for your comfort and pleasure. No cowboy would continue to ride a roping horse that would not respond to the slightest touch of the rein. It is as of great importance that a hunter be under complete control. At least half of the people who hunt are overhorsed. If you want to enjoy hunting, don't own a "spirited" horse, or at least don't mar a hunt with one. The place to break a horse is in the home pastures, not out with hounds. The person who hunts a horse that fidgets, dances, and must be kept under restraint, not only marks himself as a tyro at the game, but also causes no end of concern to other people.

Volumes are written about schooling horses to jump. My own experience has been that hunters go well that have had little experience with artificial jumps. The best one I have ever owned is a big branded grey half bred mare called "Countess" that came in from Idaho with a shipment of work stock. That day we were short of horses and so put a man upon her and told him to follow as best he could. She had never seen a rock wall nor jumps before. Hounds found and streaked away like wild geese going North. Two or three miles further at the first check, I noticed the mare standing, as quiet as a lamb. She had simply followed the other horses and jumped when they did. Nor has she refused since.

Upon another occasion in a fit of absent mindedness, I took a blood horse out that had never jumped. Immediately they were cast, hounds struck, and screamed away. Without thinking, I set the horse fast at a big rail fence and we upended and fell over it. The horse was speechless, and so was I, but with mutual apologies, we proceeded after hounds and he hit no more fences then nor later. I do not recommend the system, but it is a quick way. Once out in Texas I heard about a rancher who seemed more successful than anybody in teaching cow horses and polo ponies to stop quickly on their hindquarters, and I determined to go to see him and learn his method. Upon my arrival, he proved eager to show me the plan he had worked out. Back of the house was a long hay barn into which he led a green pony. After closing the doors at the far end, he mounted and spurred the horse into a dead run straight at the far closed doors. Just before reaching them, he sat back and shouted "Whoa." The excited pony paid no attention but plunged head on into the oak doors. Down went horse and rider in a scrambled heap.

"See," he explained, as he got up, "how I train them?" When I confessed that I didn't, he patiently elaborated the plan.

"That was only the *first* time. After the third or fourth time, they get their haunches under them, and stop when I say 'Whoa'."

There are many methods, but the natural ones are hard to beat. If you want to quickly develop a green hunter, take him hunting. A horse is herd bound by nature. He won't often stay on the wrong side of a fence when the other horses jump it. And he sees then why you want him to jump, — its to get on the other side. A school jump doesn't make sense to a horse. Years ago when my friend Marshall Derryberry bought the horse, "Star," — an animal that was to become one of the good hunters of the Middle South, he took him hunting despite the fact that the horse had never been over a jump. The first fence was worm rail, out of a pasture into a beech wood. The horse refused. All the others took it, and several riders wanted to wait for him. "Go on and leave us," shouted Marshall. A few minutes later, the horse jumped, to escape the lonesome ghost that haunts isolated horses. And, from then on, he was a made hunter. But since you will school, and are probably right, have an old veteran jumper go over the leaps ahead, and the matter of training will be acomplished in much better fashion. And start your schooling over low *solid* jumps.

Horses that are handled quietly become very fond of hunting. I had once a blood hunter, "Beloved Vagabond," that I used a great deal when hunting the "Lost River Hounds." Upon one occasion in my absence the Pack passed his stable door as they left kennels. He became greatly excited, finally jumped over the half door, trotted to his rightful place with the hounds and faithfully followed them throughout the Hunt. The general opinion seems to have been that he did better alone than he had done under my guidance.

If you are new at the game, buy a horse that has hunted five or six seasons. Don't bother too much about age, for a hunter is at his top form at around ten or twelve years. By that time he has learned the tricks of the trade; how to place himself on a bad take off, how to turn sharply where trouble yawns on the landing side, to gather speed upon an uphill approach or over water, to avoid flat limestone rocks, to place his feet in rough going, — and all the other tricks that only experience teaches. If he is up to your weight, never mind about his looks, provided his neck is long, his shoulders and pasterns sloping, and he has a fair head. Don't buy a horse until you have thoroughly tried him, and he satisfies *you*. Horses are so easy to buy, and so hard to sell! You may dislike a horse because he stepped upon your foot, or for something apparently as unrelated to the animal's real virtues, but never mind the Niagara of free advice that engulfs you. Buy a horse that you can handle with ease and that you enjoy riding. Be sure, however, that he has a fast, straight walk, and that when he is in company with other horses, he goes quietly, and doesn't "jiggle." The walk is the most important gait of a hunting horse.

Two-bits is a high price to pay for a puller. Don't buy one. If your horse develops the habit, put him to the plough for a season. Sometimes this accomplishes a lot. It is useful for most hunters. If your veterinarian says a horse is sound, don't bother about superficial blemishes. Most of the veterans carry some marks of their campaigns. "Beauty is as beauty does" in the horse world, and you will never enjoy a show hunter in the field. What you want is an old campaigner, who knows where to put his feet, and who isn't going to come down on top of you when things go wrong. Don't look at the ewe-necked, or high headed ones. Only those that carry their necks straight out, where they can study the ground ahead, are worth feeding. Disposition is the real quality that counts, and if you are ever down and tangled up with a horse, you will be grateful if you made sure above all else of a sensible disposition.

When it comes to *trading* for a horse, I am inclined to think that a young country negro from the hills back of Smiths Grove, Kentucky had received and retained the soundest advice I ever heard upon the subject. "Fat," as he was called, had a smooth, cobbed mare that could jump, and I tried to trade him a one-eyed horse and some money for her. "Fat," however, refused to trade upon any basis. He would sell, but would not take my horse in trade at any value. When I asked him why, he answered;

"I promised my po ole pappy I nevah would trade nothin' with nobody as long as I lived. You see, pappy used to swap around a lot, and finally he got him a big young, sound plow hoss, and a brand new saddle and bridle. And one day he called all us chillun into the cabin and tole us he was goin to ride down to Tennessee on a tradin' spree. An' he was goin' to keep on tradin' until he got him a fine saddle hoss and got us chillun a nice new young mammy. So he got all dressed up in his sto' clothes and rid off. Mammy was daid and they was jus' nine of us chillun home there by our selfs. So, when night come, we would latch the blind, and bolt the doah, and not come out until mawnin'. Well, that went on for five day and night, 'till we was out of meal and hongry. And then, one day, way long in the middle of the night, come a rapping at the doah. And we thought it was the ole debbil hisself, and laid low. But it was pappy, a hollering and cussing. And, when we let him in, he took the beech switch and flailed every one of us and then he said;

'Now I whopped you chullun so you could 'member this night all yoh lives. And I wants every one of you to listen to me. I rid that big, fine, young hoss off to Tennessee to trade for a saddle hoss. And I got way down below Westmoreland and trabbled around. And I heard folks say, 'Who am dat fine looking niggah on that good hoss?' And so I rid and rid, and finally I met up wid a bright skinned man, on a great big fine saddle hoss wid a yaller mane and tail. He was carrying his head and feet high and I see myself ridin' him into Glasgow looking for you chullun a new mammy. And the man say he don't want to trade, but finally I 'suaded him, by giving him my new saddle and bridle to boot. And then I forked my new hoss, and start for home. And he get slower and slower, and his head and feet git lower and lower. And finally night come and we is to the Kentucky line. And jes' as we cross de line, dat hoss stick his haid down and drap dead.'

'Now chullun,' he said 'Heah you pappy home, hongry and he ain't got no hoss, no new saddle and no bridle. And you chullun ain't got no nice young mammy. So I'm going to brush you wid de beech once mo', — to 'press on you I don't want none of you to nevah trade nothin' with nobody as long as you lives, — and no time with nobody from Tennessee'."

Man is a strange animal for he consistently overfeeds himself and his horses, and underfeeds his hounds. The average hunter needs one quart of oats per-mile of daily work. If he is exercised four miles a day, four days, and hunts twenty miles a day twice a week, 8 quarts a day (in a limestone country) is about right. If he is used by a Huntsman or a Whip, he may need another gallon a day added to this ration, or a similar increase if he is a "first flighter's" mount and really gallops.

Sons or grandsons of landowners.

CHAPTER XIV

THE LANDOWNER

Most foxhunters are landowners, or the sons or grandsons of landowners, for the sport is essentially a rural one. If played in the near suburbia of large cities it must be liberally subsidized, and kept alive by the constant infusion of hard money. The laws of almost all states amply protect the right of foxhounds to cross land in pursuit of their game. But only the sufferance of the farmer, or of the landowner, makes it possible to follow hounds across the country. Oddly enough, at least in the South, custom decrees that following hounds is not trespassing and very few farmers object to hunters crossing their land. While all good foxhunters live in the country, few of them own or control enough land to hunt for any great part of the time across their own acres. Many wolf hunters in the West, and some grey fox chasers in the deep South never have to leave their own ranches or plantations. But in red fox country, the situation is different. To begin with, red foxes prefer rich land, bluegrass land by choice. They leave the scrub oak and thin country to the greys. Now men who follow the red fox rarely seem to accumulate vast territories of rich land. And they are all dependent upon the friendliness of, not only their neighbors, but of everybody within many miles. So it is essential, if you intend to be a good foxhunter, that you so live as to gain and hold the respect of everybody in your community. This means that you lead a decent kind of a life, and that you be careful and considerate of the other fellow, his property, his fences, his stock, his fields and his beliefs. If you are, he will meet you three-quarters of the way.

  The man whose lot in life is to live in town misses many things of value, but the greatest thing he misses is the unselfish, warmhearted friendliness of the countryman. The man who makes his living from the land, be he old or young, rich or poor, black or white, has something in his soul untainted by the struggle of the marketplace. He is almost always willing to lend a hand to the fellow whose ox is in the ditch. To him a neighbor is not a competitor, but is a fellow being who takes the sun and the rain as he does, and who has some part with him in the misfortune of a bad season, and in the plenty of a good one. And to share a little of this gentle and kindly attitude towards life is the richest reward of foxhunting. When I think of the men over whose land I have ridden for uncounted years, I grow humble in my heart, for I owe much happiness to them. One man comes always first to my mind. For many years we hunted across his lands, and times without number met at his place. And always he waited at the gate and greeted each foxhunter with a welcome so sincere and gentle that every man, woman, or child who met him was wrapped in a cloak of friendliness. John A. Holt, — has "crossed over Jordan," but the warmth of his kindly heart will linger long over his community. All the Holts are cut from priceless cloth, and whoever comes to chase the fox over their fields and great hills, meets always the same gentle welcome. Old county families, the people who have held their lands against Indians, taxes, wars and depressions, are the real friends of hunting, just as they are the foundation of everything sound and true in our way of life. In our county the names are straight out of the "Doomsday Book," — Herbert, Williams, Puryear, Phillips, Primm, Cook, Knox, Fly, Edmondson . . . good names carried by good men. If the landowners in your hunting country carry similar names, then all you have to do is to make sure that you do your part — they will certainly do theirs.

  Five or six times a season is enough to hunt over any one piece of land. This means that a two day a week country should encompass at least eighty square miles, and more, if possible. In these days of trailers and trucks, it is no great inconvenience to meet forty miles from the kennel. This is helpful in many ways, it not only relieves pressure upon a small country, but enables you to pick out particularly good hunting grounds over wider areas. Everybody likes to vary the hunting scene now and then, and there is an unfailing charm to a country that is a little strange.

When you are going to hunt in a new territory, you should always get some representative citizen to go with you, and to call upon the landholders a week or two in advance. If you do this, you will be welcomed, and if you fail to do it, you are not likely to be invited back. Never forget under any circumstances that you are a guest of the man who owns the land. It is his kindness that makes your hunting possible. And presently you may discover, as so many of us have, that his friendship is one of foxhunting's greatest rewards.

THE COUNTRY

When a boy grows to be a man and starts questing for a mate, he may range no further than his own district and, having espied a yellow haired girl with blue eyes,

". . . take what Fate or the Gods may give,
ask no question and make no prayer . . ."

Or he may seek the wide world over intent upon finding the combination of beauty and saint that beckons him in dreams. So it is with a hunting country, you may accept what is at hand and make the best of it, or search before you settle, and mayhap escape a lifetime of regrets.

If there is a fair country adjacent, and a good country available across the county, take the better one, regardless of the distance and inconvenience. Many men accept the country they live in and are shackled the remainder of their lives.

What constitutes a good country? Broadly speaking any country has merit if an average man upon a good horse can stay with hounds in the major portion of it. And there are comparatively few such countries hunted in the United States today. Perhaps it might be useful to first point out the features that mar a country. The most common ones are:

1. Large wooded hills.
2. Rivers, creeks, or cliff forming small streams.
3. Extensive areas of woodlands, marshlands, or unrideable territory.

4. Highways.
5. Unjumpable fences.

A country may look good but if in it there is a range of wooded hills it is *there* that the fox will run, and not over the bright meadows. If there is a single isolated hill here and there and it is separated from its neighbor by a couple of miles, foxes will run across the good country from one hill to another. If there is a river forming a boundary, Brother Fox will hie him to its banks and cliffs at the first cry of a feathering hound. And even smaller streams, with extensive cliffs, or steep clay banks, will make it at times impossible to stay with hounds. I know one country of large grass fields, gentle slopes and jumpable fences that is bisected by a mild looking creek of modest size, but with clay banks and few fords. To *look* at the country I would think it wonderful, but a huntsman who rode it for many years told me that three foxes out of four ran the stream banks and time without number left the Field upon the wrong side. Unless a stream is readily fordable at frequent intervals it is a potent obstacle.

It is unnecessary to comment upon the death toll of a highway. A railway is not nearly so great a problem, for there are fewer trains than trucks. Unjumpable fences are familiar enough to us all. They constitute a terrific handicap, but hounds do get through, under, or over them, even though the toll is a ghastly one. Also the weight of these barriers upon your selection of a hunting country would be measured by your capacity to panel, gate and modify the fences.

We have discussed the factors that ruin or mar, so perhaps it might be worthwhile to describe the features of a good country. It should be gently rolling, with large enclosures, and small isolated covers. And it should not be a small grain country, or it will be taboo to cross it in season. Above all it must be rideable.

Now if we are in search of better country we want grass, — *blue-grass*. This to me is the 'sine qua non' of hunting; first, because it is beautiful, second, because a firm old blue-grass sod is so marvelous to gallop over, and third, because grass holds scent so well.

Climate must be given serious thought if we are in search of a hunting Elysium. The best hunting climate is that of Middle Tennessee, because it is windless and so mild that the frost rarely interferes. However, perhaps there is no hunting country on this earth that can compare, despite its colder climate, with extensive areas in the blue-grass regions of Kentucky, that lay back from the river or the bordering hills. Between Winchester, Paris, and Mt. Sterling is probably the world's best hunting country, — if we shut our eyes to the present fences. Here is an area perhaps twenty miles square, eighty percent of which is in sod a century old, and so firm that a horse hardly marks it even after a heavy rain. The enclosures are generally large. Fields of one hundred acres are quite prevalent, and larger ones by no means scarce. Livestock and tobacco are the crops and neither small grain nor corn fields mar the scene. Cover is small and scarce, but these are pasture-bred foxes and rely upon straight speed rather than stratagem. From such a country the great hounds should continue to develop, — if they can learn to handle the woven-wire fences.

It is difficult to tell much about a country by driving through it, because one can look across sharp valleys and never see them. To be sure that a country is suitable for hunting you must first hunt it enough to know. And no one should take a country as a permanent proposition until he is quite confident that it is the best available, for upon this one decision hangs the measure of his contentment during long years, or even for a lifetime.

They drink the headiest drafts that man can quaff.

CHAPTER XV

RIDING TO HOUNDS

There are a lot of ways of riding to hounds, but it doesn't make any real difference how you ride. If you do enough of it, you will ride well whether you ride bare-back upon a mule, or use a "Whippy" upon a descendant of Lexington. A long time ago, when the "forward seat" had just been introduced to this country by the Milanese, a cavalry officer, fresh from the Mounted Service School, arrived in Lexington and rode out one morning with me to hunt with Sam Wooldridge's hounds. As we jogged down the lanes toward the Kentucky River side of the country, the Major opened upon the subject of the new Italian style of riding.

"What seat do you ride, Mr. Wooldridge?" he asked in his best academic manner.

"What did you say," said Sam, who was totally indifferent to the technical verbiage of the riding academy. The major explained for the ensuing half hour, and finally pointed out that in a country full of such sharp declivities, it would be impossible for a man to do any job at all following hounds unless he understood the use of the "forward seat." Sam grunted acquiescence, and presently hounds struck and were away along a "hog back" that ended on the top of old "Fort" Hill. The hounds checked there, then picked up the line half way down, and swept into the valley with everything from the clarinet to the bass drum sounding. From a horse's back, the down slope of "Fort" Hill looks like a precipice. You can, however, with care *lead* a horse down it. With a wild whoop of encouragement to "Big Stride," Sam was away down the place at a *gallop*. The Major went over his horse's head a little way down and we never saw him again. Whether he still lies there with the Indians who fell long ago in the battle, or whether he caught his horse and returned to the world to expound upon the use of the new seat, none of us ever knew. We caught up finally with the Wooldridge seat sometime thereafter, and had a glorious day.

To have stout hearted riders on each side of you and nothing but sod between you and hounds, is to be in one of the greatest situations on earth. Where your heels and hands are is a matter of no immediate consequence. You need not even make a pretense of good riding, yet still may see a lot of the chase and have a lot of fun. Hunting is an amusement and not a college board examination. A fox hunter is at perfect liberty to pursue the methods that best please him, to ride the roads, to look for the gaps in the fences, to mark the course of the hounds and cut across the fields to them, or to sit and listen. Some go hunting solely for the pleasure of a hard ride over stiff fences. More power to them! If they like it and can do it, there is no wine that carries greater stimulation. That instant in eternity when a horse is in the air over a fence sets a man's soul free. And if the bold crowd the hounds now and then, let's not curse them. Age and caution cry their line in pursuit and will all too soon pull them down. Besides, as Conan Doyle's French captain said when he rode over a hound; "After all, one must break the shell to get at the egg." All hunt because they love the out-of-doors, the crisp air, and the pleasure of meeting old friends. And, the brave have an added love — the pulse quickening passion of danger. But if you are too old to leap fences, it is after all as much pleasure to see a fox found, as to see him put to ground. And perhaps more pleasure to see hounds work out a bad loss than either. All of us know people who can identify every hound, every low place in the fences, every by-lane, the safe creek crossings, and every fox's run. And they can get across the country with the ease and quietness of a fox. If I may be forgiven for praising the lady who has tolerated my faults for the past quarter of a century, I can illustrate what such wise hunters accomplish. The Harpeth Hills are wooded, very rough, and full of stout foxes. And it takes a hard rider on a good horse to stay in hearing of hounds when a fox runs through such Grampian slopes. Upon one occasion, we hit a fox that winged his way over the hills like a wild goose. Through woods, up and down hills, over the wire and rocks, we pressed far behind the pack until finally ahead upon a rocky slope, we sighted a familiar piebald mare surrounded by hounds. Our spent horses at last toiled up the eminence and there, at the foxes' den, was Sara, tightening a loose hind shoe with a rock. Few of us will ever forget that lesson. When the chase started we had gone "hell for leather" after hounds, up hill and down dale, over rocks and through dense woods, and our arrival at the den was a great triumph of brawn over the matter. But my lady had borrowed an idea or two from the foxes in her long hunting experience and so had upon this and many other occasions charted her own course. There are more ways than one to cross a country after hounds.

The best thing to do if you are new either to the hunting game or to the country is to pick out a leader, someone who knows the country and rides in moderation. Then, give your guide plenty of room, thirty or forty yards, and you will not make a nuisance of yourself. The first time I ever hunted with the Limerick Hounds in Ireland, I was quite apprehensive of my ability to cope with the banks and looked about the Field for a conservative to follow. Just then I spotted Mr. W. E. Grogan who had been twenty years Master of the Carlow and came occasionally to hunt with the Limerick. He was then, I believe, in his seventieth year. Surely, I thought, I can follow a man who spots me thirty years! Hounds quickly found in a small gorse cover and streamed away across a great vale like arrows in flight. Away went Mr. Grogan, and I followed. The walls were low, the sod sound and the going wonderful. But, as we swept into the vale, the fields grew larger and the walls higher and higher until presently, barring the way ahead, there reared across our course a great monadnock of a wall. I knew my horse couldn't make it and thought Mr. Grogan must know a place to get over. But he neither looked to the right nor the left! I blinked, and shuddered. He was over! Then, I felt my horse rise, — we were on top of the wall, off and away again. In answer, I suppose, to my prayers, hounds checked in that field. Still shaking, I rode up to my guide and vouchsafed the opinion that it was a stiff piece of country we had just come over.

"Was it?" replied Mr. Grogan and blinked his mild blue eyes. "You know, my glasses came off at the first jump and I could never see the other ones."

If you find yourself alone in a strange country, "patience does it." Stop and listen. If you don't hear hounds, be patient and listen again and again. Sooner or later, upon an ordinary occasion, the cry of hounds will reach you.

138 "GONE AWAY!"

Many fences must be led over.

Don't get in a hurry now, but wait and see if you can mark their direction. And then, make your way towards them. Remember that a hunted fox generally runs a circle and if you get the direction he is making, you can frequently intercept his arc not far behind hounds. But don't ride aimlessly. Wait until sound or inquiry has revealed the direction of the hounds. The one rule of the rider who stays with hounds is, "get to cry." If it's a crack pack and harbors no "dwellers," nor hounds that cry a covered line, this rule will, nine times out of ten, suffice to keep him "upon speaking terms" with hounds. But, in much of the wire maze that does duty as hunting country today, getting to hounds calls for no inconsiderable skill and ingenuity. Many fences must be led over. Where two riders can dismount and stand on the wire while others lead the horses over, there is no great problem. But when you are alone and must both stand on the wire and coax your horse over it, the problem becomes one that requires some horse training. Horses don't see wire fences well enough to jump them, unless the wire is marked by a sapling, brush or a coat. Most of the horses that hunt with the Hillsboro Hounds learned long ago to jump a coat over wire, and will do so with ease and precision. Don't face your horse when leading over an obstacle, for that confuses him. Now and then, horses are trained so that they will follow their owner and jump after him. If you hunt west of Middleburg, Virginia and plan to stay near hounds, you must school your horse to be quiet when tangled in wire, for he will have to be cut out of it many times.

If you want to stay close to hounds, you must, however, figure upon some falls. This is a subject which the writer feels amply qualified to discuss with authority. Falling from a horse looks much more dangerous than it is. As a matter of fact, there is very little danger of it, — not half as much as walking across a modern highway. To begin with, you don't really fall from the height of the saddle on an upright horse. If you go over his head, he is probably either on his knees, or nearly so. If you fall to the side, you lose contact generally when only two or three feet from the ground. You may get shaken up a bit, and now and then somebody gets a finger broken but actually bathtubs produce more bad accidents than good hunting horses. The trouble is only when people ride fool horses that plunge and kick when they get into difficulties. Roll free of such animals when they go down. Keep rolling when you hit the ground and you will be all right. Of course, you don't need to fall hardly at all if you don't want to, for you may acquire a good, well-mannered hunter and jump only where there is a decent takeoff and landing. Then you ask only a reasonable performance of your horse and lastly jump at a moderate pace. Most jumping is over timber, or an occasional wall, so there is no reason to approach at much speed. Use a hunting breastplate, and hang on to it if you are insecure. You shouldn't fall off a *well-schooled good* horse if you do this.

The secret of falling is to hang on as long as you can before you let go. And, don't turn loose the reins at all, if you can help it. If falling would kill, the writer would have long since been dead. Most falls are nothing but a roll in the grass, or mud on a coat. Nothing is better for a beginner than a fall. He discovers that there is little to it, and his confidence mounts immediately.

Nobody is looking for falls for they do muddy up boots, but with reasonable care about picking jumpable places and sensible mounts, the ordinary rider in a hunting field rarely has one. A man hunting hounds or riding Whip, of course, expects them. Let your horse have his head as he takes off, keep your weight forward, and you will rarely come down. If you don't come forward with your horse as he rises, the movement tends to whip you in that direction, disturbs your balance, and if the horse pecks on landing, you are easily unseated. The secret of avoiding falls is to "lay off the pace," and to "look before you leap."

Of course, if you hunt with a "country pack," like the "Hillsboro," you are forever creeping up and down banks, weaving through trees, removing wild grape vines and greenbriars from around your throat, jumping into brambles, turning on a dime to avoid a precipice, stumbling over hidden wire and galloping across rocks that would sink a steamboat, but, none of this occasions serious tumbles. If you don't hang your stirrup upon a gatepost, and if your horse will jump at the exact place you want him to, hunting, even in a wilderness, is less dangerous than Badminton.

There are a few simple things to bear in mind when crossing a country. When fording a stream, look for a place that farm wagons once used, or better, still use. Failing that, look for gravel bars and wind your way across them. Of course, rocky ledges are even safer. Give your horse his head when he is crossing slick rocks, and he won't come down. In wet, ploughed ground, ride the furrows where the water lies for it is firmer there. If you cannot keep to the furrow, cross ridge and furrow at an angle. When you must cross grain fields, hug the headlands, and you may hunt again on that farm. Jump the low places in the fence when you can. Walk and trot your horse, when you can do so without losing ground. Get off him at a check, if you have had a fast go. He will go farther and faster the oftener you rid him of your weight. Use lanes, trails and paths whenever they go your way. The packed ground is easier for your horse. In bottom land, hug the line of trees that border the stream for the ground is higher and firmer there. Go slantwise up steep hills and, if they are long ones, also zig-zag upwards. It will save your horse. Through thick woodlands, keep an eye out for old logging roads and game trails and follow them as much as you can. Go fast at the uphill leaps and slowly at the downhill ones. When the ground dips towards the jump have a care, and find another place if you can. It's easy for a horse to hang his kees with such a takeoff. Approach water and ditches with some speed, for you can't clear such places unless you do. Many people in a country like Tennessee become so accustomed to jumping in close places that they approach clear rail and rock fences very slowly and let a horse take off from too close a position. At heights from three and a half feet up, a horse should have a little gallop at his fences. It's easier then for both him and you.

"Look before you leap" ought to be engraven upon the lintels of every stable door in the "natural" countries. An artificial jump is only put at safe places, but upon the other side of an old stone wall there may be a rock quarry. Make the pace over firm going and save your horse over the soft ground. When you hit a farm lane or a road that leads towards hounds, make up for lost time. If a wind is blowing and you can't hear hounds, turn down wind, — that's probably what the fox did.

Keep away from churches, there may be special services of some kind going on. Don't wait to learn this the hard way. We ran a fox through the "Grove" Churchyard once with twenty couple of hounds in full cry. The men in the congregation all came to the doors. Not content with the sacrilege, an hour later Br'er Fox repeated the route, this time right under the windows. The music of the pack made a falsetto out of the organ's efforts and every man ran out of the church and cheered. Two months later, I was searching for a lost hound in the neighborhood and asked a farmer's wife to use the telephone.

"No." she flared, "You are the man whose hounds broke up our meeting." It took a year for us to re-establish ourselves in the community.

If I could be granted just one wish, it would be that the wire, — the horrible, rusted, entangling blight be removed from our fields. It has no place in life and, like the steel trap, harbors only laceration and pain. Once a long time ago, I was on an antelope hunt in the Texas Panhandle, and attended a very delightful sportsmen's dinner given by the principal ranchers of that then wild country. When called upon for a toast, I fervently offered a youthfully exuberant prayer that the man who invented fence wire be eternally dammed. No one drank but me, and in sable silence, I shrunk into my seat. As we rode home that night, my host gently informed me that the rancher upon my right at the table was the son of the inventor of fence wire.

If you and I are to hunt, we must meet the stuff, for the rock walls are falling, the rail fences crumbling, and the wire is creeping like a snake into Eden. So, hate it as we all do who cherish the beauty of the countryside, nothing remains for us to do but to face it, and to devise ways to get our hounds through and our horses over it. With my generation, who can remember an almost unmarred world of rail and wall, the wire is a "bete noir" that haunts our dreams. However, I am cheered at times by two of my hunting companions,* for to them wire is hardly more than greenbriars, and undismayed, they drag it off posts, stomp it to the ground or pile brush against it, so quickly that the whole operation snatches but an instant from the staccato thunder of their horses' hoofs on the sod.

The best man** I have ever seen behind hounds, taking any and all kinds of country into consideration, has not only a "long head" but also a grand pair of ears. The most distant cry records for him a message of both direction and speed, and at the sound, he is away like a flash in the right direction. Nor does he linger undecided about the route. As he gallops on, he must have usually charted his course, for he does not often put himself in cul-de-sacs nor face long detours. Such a rider looks ahead at the country whenever hounds check, and maps possible courses in his mind, noting the openings, and calculating the route of the fox. The man who stays near hounds in an average natural country today must not only ride his own line, but must think ahead all the time. "If the fox turns to that woodland, I will make for the gate, double back, jump in and out of that hog pen, leap the wire fence where the honeysuckle is thick upon it . . . or, if he turns back up that branch as he did last time, I will jump back out on that lane, gallop to that farmyard gate, jump the old rail fence beyond it, and be in that big pasture with the hounds . . ." This is the sort of navigation that is required of a "first flighter" today. Judgment of course is vital to all pursuits and some form of it, at least, is helpful to the fellow who would like to long engage in the sport of riding to hounds. Many riders feel that experience at

---

* Robert Harwell and Henry Bell Covington.
** John Sloan, Esq.

so simple a pastime is of little consequence; but, "he jests at scars who never felt a wound" and knowledge, patiently gained, can be extremely useful when hounds stream away into a strange country. However, a slight touch of courage is probably the most useful luggage you can carry to journey with hounds. Those lads and lassies, whose hearts are always over the next fence, are the real fox hunters. The cry of the hounds ahead sets the blood tingling in their veins, and they shed caution and care as freely as a cottonwood tree sheds leaves. They drink the headiest draughts that men can quaff, and for them, when the pack flies forward in full cry, there are high wild notes of music that other ears can never hear.

Mason Houghland, M.F.H. Painted by Goode Davis.

EPILOGUE

Then, after many blunders and years, *you* stand pentitent, hat in hand, at the Judgment Seat. And the Judge says,

"Does this mean that after a half century of trying, you couldn't even develop a pack of good hounds?" You will, perhaps, defend yourself and explain that in youth you read this book, and it was wrong, and threw you off the right line. Then, Saint Peter will probably say:

"Let the punishment fall instead upon the author of the book!" The Recording Angel will doubtless take his quill from behind his ear, lean forward, and in a whisper, remind the Saint of the new regulations:

"P 47256, Y3: *All* foxhunters to go straight to Hell, — for they have had their Heaven on Earth."

Gone Away.

3/01

799.25 Houghland, Mason.
HOU
Gone away

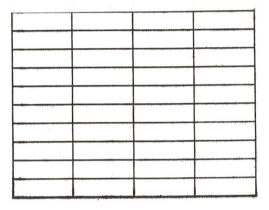

GILES COUNTY PUBLIC LIBRARY
PULASKI, TENNESSEE 38478

GAYLORD M2